STOLEN CHILDHOOD

What You Need to Know about Sexual Abuse

Alice Huskey

INTERVARSITY PRESS
DOWNERS GROVE, ILLINOIS 60515

InterVarsity Press is the book publishing division of InterVarsity Christian Fellowship, a student
movement active on campus at hundreds of universities, colleges and schools of nursing in the
United States of America, and a member movement of the International Fellowship of Evangelical
Students. For information about local and regional activities, write Public Relations Dept.,
InterVarsity Christian Fellowship, 6400 Schroeder Rd., P.O. Box 7895, Madison, WI 53707-7895.

Distributed in Canada through InterVarsity Press, 860 Denison St., Unit 3, Markham, Ontario
L3R 4H1, Canada.

ISBN 0-8308-1216-4

Printed in the United States of America ∞

Library of Congress Cataloging-in-Publication Data
Huskey, Alice, 1943-
    Stolen childhood / Alice Huskey.
      p.   cm.
    Includes bibliographical references.
    ISBN 0-8308-1216-4
    1. Child molesting—United States.   2. Child molesting—Religious
aspects—Christianity.   3. Child molesters—United States.
4. Sexually abused children—Services for—United States.
I. Title.
HQ72.U53H87   1990   90-37416
362.7'6—dc20   CIP

12   11   10 9 8 7 6 5 4 3 2 1
99   98   97 96 95 94 93 92 91 90

*For my mother
who believed me
and took steps
to get help*

–1–

A
Painful
Introduction

_____

*F*ear *and relief gripped my body as I cautiously peered* through the kitchen window. Two deputy sheriffs were leading my father away. He glanced angrily over his shoulder toward the house. His lips seemed to form the message "I'll kill you." It was not the last time he would voice that threat.

The past ten years of my life had been filled with secrets, but I had finally told my mother the most dreadful secret of all.

Mother had just returned home from several days away on a nursing job. She was excited about our friends' new baby and was interested in news about home. The conversation seemed normal. But suddenly, without planning, I told her that my father had slept with me. Quickly her excitement turned to distress, and she left the house abruptly.

The day turned into an unbelievable nightmare. I stood alone that hot July day, shocked, dazed, numbed by fear. I feared what I had said to upset my mother, feared her leaving me, feared her punishing me. I feared my father returning home only to find out that Mother now knew about us. When Mother returned, she said she had gone to some friends and that we should go to the county sheriff. New fears gripped me. As frightened as I was of my father, I was even more frightened of the police!

Instead of feeling the relief of finally disclosing my secret, I found that my mind was churning with questions. What had my father done? What had I done? What will happen now? Why did my mother tell someone else, especially the sheriff, what I had said? What was she thinking? What will happen to her? What will she do to me? Why is she so afraid? What will my father do to me?

At the sheriff's office, we waited for what seemed forever. And then the officers asked me endless questions of their own. Along with the questions came warnings not to talk about certain things outside their office. That made my mind reel. More secrets! And the message "Tell the truth, but don't tell the truth." I was tired of covering up. I began to worry that I would be punished or even sent to jail.

As we returned home, my fears overwhelmed me. I knew my father would soon come home from work. My main question became "What will he do to me?" He could get so angry!

The time until he returned home was tense. The kitchen window had always been my lookout post as I waited for my father to come home to use me. Now, through the same window, I watched my father scuffle with the police and be led away in handcuffs.

Little did I know what effect my disclosure would have on the rest of my life. In a sense, my ordeal had just begun.

The Beginnings of Abuse

I can hardly recall a time before the abuse. I can vaguely remember waking up one morning when I was about three years old and finding my pajama bottoms off. I was puzzled, but then I remembered my father removing them during the night and my telling him that *I* would put them back on myself.

What seemed so inconsequential grew into painful memories. My life became bound by secrets and fear. I really did not understand what was happening to me. When Mother worked nights, my father would come to my bed or carry me off to theirs. His sexual demands varied, but they all left me gagging and feeling suffocated, nauseated or petrified by fear and pain. I experienced endless torture as he tried to penetrate me. I hated the sticky mess I was left to clean up.

The brief sessions at night grew into long nights, weekends and evenings. With the rest of the family at church, I was his prey on Sunday and Wednesday evenings. Then he started abusing me almost daily after work.

Sometimes I would pretend I was asleep. I tried to fade into the wall. Other times I fought to get away from him, refusing his rewards of ice cream for strange, bizarre behavior. But nothing helped.

I really did not understand what was happening to me. I was only a child being exposed prematurely to adult behavior. My father had developed a pattern with me which I now know as "incest." Because I was a child, I didn't have an adult's physical, mental or psychological defenses. Because I feared him, I couldn't tell anyone.

Obeying my parents had been instilled in me since infancy. I was to love and honor them. At the same time I had been taught not to lie, yet I had been frightened into lying to keep my father's secret. It was all so confusing to me, more than I could sort out on my own.

Oh, I asked my father why he was making me do things with him that I hated. He would reply that he was teaching me, and this was "the right way it was done with people." He insisted I not question him. I was to obey and trust him. He would look after my best interests.

But I had a hard time believing my father! I received so many conflicting messages, resulting in ambivalent feelings. I was supposed to enjoy it, but I didn't. It was supposed to be okay, but I had to keep it a secret. It didn't make sense. No one at school ever talked about anything like this. If it was so "normal," why didn't my mother talk about it?

Curiosity got the better of me at times. I searched for adoption papers, thinking I could not belong to these parents if such a thing was happening to me. I searched the house for evidence and found devices and books which only intensified my fear and guilt.

Relief came the year my younger brother was born. My grandmother came to visit, and I begged to go home with her. It started as a happy year. I enjoyed spending time with my newborn cousin and receiving the loving care of my grandmother and aunts. But the reprieve was short-lived. Another relative visited and he too expected sex from me. Soon I could hardly bear to be with a male relative. This worsened when I accidentally opened the bathroom door and saw my uncle exposed. When I returned home the next year, my father started to use me again— with my young brother in the same room, possibly watching.

There were times that I could not get past my father's bribes. For instance, there was the morning of my eleventh birthday. I had finally talked my mother into a birthday party. I had not had one for many years. She said to get things straightened up before my guests arrived, and she would be home in time to conduct the party. Little did my mother know that my father would not let me get ready for the party until I had given him a "gift." Another day he brought presents for both my mother and me. I tried to refuse, knowing what it meant, but Mother insisted on my being thankful for the present.

But my father was capable of using violence as well as gifts to control me. I often saw him physically abusing my brothers. I knew the imprint of his slap on my face. Watching him hit Mother even once crushed me emotionally! Needless to say, I had a tremendous fear of my father and his quick temper. When my father said "I'll skin you alive," as he often did, I was sure he meant it. I could picture the results in my mind. The effect was emotional dynamite. I was terrified at the thought of anything happening to me or those I loved.

And then one day a boy told me that he knew what my father was doing to me. With that, the boy threatened to tell my father he knew—unless I would let him do the same things. He said no one would know, especially not my father. I did not want to give in, but I did anyway. I didn't like it, and I knew it was wrong, but I felt powerless.

One thing led to another, and soon unwanted actions became habits, routine patterns in my life. It seemed as if all the boys in the neighborhood knew and expected the same sexual privileges. What I had first done to save myself from my father's anger soon robbed me of any sense of safety I might have had. At the same time, even though I did not like my involvement with these boys, I had a sense of being accepted by them. But what a price to pay!

One day the boys chose to use me in the restroom of a nearby park. I hated lying outstretched on the cold, filthy floor, being used over and over again. Finally, the father of one of the boys came to find his son. How vividly I remember the double guilt: guilt for telling him nothing had happened and guilt for knowing what *had* happened.

I never considered telling Mother or anyone else about my abuse and pain. As a matter of fact, I was terrified when twice I thought my mother had found out!

The first time was when I started menstruating. My parents confronted me together about the stained clothing my mother had found. Mother had become curious when my underclothes gradually disappeared. She never knew how long I had kept them hidden. In a way, their confrontation was a relief because I learned the cause of the bleeding. Even though I had just found out the facts of life, I had assumed this bleeding was a result of my involvement with my father, perhaps a punishment from God. I didn't try to tell my mother the truth. How could I ever have managed it in my father's angry presence? There was just no way that I could explain.

The other incident was soon after that, when my mother took me
to a female doctor. I had never had such a thorough examination. It
was so hard for me to answer the doctor's questions, especially when
she asked me if I ever bled. I lied, anxiously certain she knew my
secret. Would she tell Mother? I felt so sick to my stomach just
anticipating what might happen to me. But nothing did; I'm not sure
why.

Aftermath of Disclosure
But then, at thirteen, I had blurted out the secret myself! There was
nothing I could do now but bear the consequences. Mother reacted in
shock, but managed to do the right thing. Most importantly she believed me. And then she took action.

I wondered what would happen next. Sure enough, it was in the
newspaper the next day. Even though it was a small article, I was
sure everyone would read of my secret. What would they think?

It seemed as if some of my mother's friends at church were supportive, but it was so painful to hear snatches of gossip at church and
in the community. I remember going to the church picnic and wanting
only to stay close to my mother. She was all I had and I needed her.
But she wanted to talk alone with her friends, and she shooed me
away. I didn't understand that she needed to talk to her friends too.
I didn't want to leave her side because I was afraid. I felt as if I had
a big sign around my neck saying "dirty, ugly, naughty, guilty—stay
away."

It seemed like there were so many unwanted phone calls and ha-
rassments. Others in the community avoided us. I called the one
friend I had to see if I could visit. She did not understand what had
happened to me, even after reading the newspaper. But her parents
did. Even as I sat on the curb talking with her, I felt all alone, without
friends.

Over the years, I had isolated myself socially as a protective shield.
After disclosing the abuse, I was sure no one would like me. And

what's more, I was convinced I didn't deserve friends after what I had done.

The days and weeks that followed my disclosure seemed so long, yet meshed together in my mind. I was panicked when my father was let out on bond. With his temper I would easily be a target of revenge. He was a man of his word.

The night he was released Mother went to church to try to continue "normal routine." I was left at home with a friend. When I heard what was either the backfire of a passing car or gunshot, it escalated my fear. Even after help came that night, it did not alleviate the longing I had for safety. I never *really* felt safe.

A few days later, the school nurse interrupted my third day of eighth grade. She very cautiously escorted me to a house near my home. From there I was taken by police car to protective custody, connected with juvenile hall. I couldn't even wear my own clothes. I had to wait for an older "inmate" to sift through the donated clothing to see what she thought might fit me. The institutional garb, physical examination and locked doors added to my feeling like a criminal. I felt so filthy! And my fears of jail had been founded on truth!

Though it was supposed to be "protective custody," it felt like punishment. I had to obey orders and think and behave the way others did, even when policies were foreign to what I believed. I felt pushed to conform to others' routines and standards just the way my father pushed me to do what I did not want to do. Any nonconformity or expression of emotion, even boredom or depression, resulted in what seemed like solitary confinement. (Today I can understand that the purpose of taking everything away and having the staff constantly monitor me was to make sure that I did not hurt myself out of desperation or despondency.)

I would hear remarks from the staff like "The courts don't believe little girls, they believe adults." My situation seemed hopeless!

During my time in custody, I took many psychological tests, but received no counseling. (What did they want to know, anyway, with those crazy inkblots!) I decided to look for my own counselor. I tried talking with the student chaplain but found no solace or relief from my guilt. I felt so distant from God. I was sure God saw me as a spiritual failure!

Then came the trial itself. *Devastating* is the only word to explain it. Usually I had to wear institutional clothing to court, and I hoped all the while that no one would recognize me. Unfortunately, the first judge was from my hometown. Even if he hadn't been, I still would have felt conspicuous. There were so many people attending the trial.

After that I went to a number of courts, always in custody. I felt badgered by all those men who asked questions. They all wanted specific details. I never knew who, if anyone, was on my side. How could I answer with a simple yes or no to their statements when they used phrases and words totally unfamiliar to me?

My father had abused me so many times for so many years. How was I to remember the exact dates, times and duration evidently needed to establish a case? How could I remember at least ten years of abuse to which I had tried to deaden my feelings and thoughts in order to escape the disgrace and pain? I had no real concept of time and events. All I knew was what my father had told me. All I had was a child's view of an overwhelming relationship with her father. I became more and more certain that *I* was the one in trouble and the punishment had already begun.

My father got off with only a short stay in custody for observation. (Even so, he verbally threatened my life as he left the courtroom.) I don't think I got off as easy. I came away from the hearings and trials feeling even more unloved, unlovable and guilty. Not wanting to do anything else to hurt my mother, I decided to stay away from her. And so, when given the choice, I begged to live in a foster home—a self-inflicted punishment. In my mind there was no way my mother could love me after I broke up our home and sent her husband to jail.

My mother chose the foster home, and the authorities approved it. Gramma (my foster mom) had also taken care of me when I was a baby. She and her family provided the loving setting I needed so much in the next few months.

I felt that I was making a fresh start—until a probation officer came to see me at school one day. How embarrassing! I was sure everyone would know about my past, and I'd been so careful to keep it a secret. It was so hard trying to explain to my newfound friends about this visitor.

The probation officer brought a gift. I loved gifts, but not this one. It was a size-forty sweater, totally unsuitable for an underdeveloped, hundred-pound thirteen-year-old. It hurt to receive a gift that proved once more that no one really knew me or my needs. The officer only came one other time, and I had no way of contacting her, even if I needed or wanted to do so.

Picking Up the Pieces

After spending about nine months away from my mother, I returned to live with her. By then my parents were divorced. I had vowed that I would make things up to my mother and talk to her about everything. I remember going to her bedside that first night, asking if we could be close. She didn't respond the way I had expected. Things were not the way I'd hoped they would be.

I started high school, only to have my high-school peers heap guilt on me. They had not forgotten the story. In a way, my absence had brought on even more gossip. I could not believe my ears when someone finally told me what everyone assumed: I had gone away to have a baby! Knowing it wasn't true didn't give me peace; I wanted to be believed. The situation was worse than my wildest expectations.

Adolescence is a time to select and refine life values. My circumstances led to unbalanced, unhealthy results. Social rejection increased my poor socializing skills, guilt and self-protection. I further isolated myself from my peers, blaming all my problems on them. Underneath I longed for friends and a place in a group. I was desperate for peer acceptance.

I dated guys from other towns so they would not know my past. I wanted so to be close and loved, but all I knew was sexual closeness. I rejected older dates who wanted only sex, but tried to find sexual closeness with younger males I really cared for. I would have done anything for them to accept me. I'm thankful now that God placed males with strong moral standards in my life who did not give in to my seductive ways.

I thought perfect grades in school would help me gain recognition, so I earned A's in every subject except physical education. My hard work got me nowhere, even with my mother. So I tried to get low grades to get in with another peer group. That didn't work either. I only kept myself from forming adequate study habits. On the surface it appeared as though I was trying, but I never felt worthy of achieving.

Moral and value decisions were important to me. I spent a lot of time involved in church youth groups, Bible quiz team and other church activities. Yet for all my religious activity, I still felt so immoral inside.

I felt guilty for disobeying my father by betraying him, especially in court. But I was being truthful. When my father sent me a birthday card with a verse about children obeying parents, I felt even more guilty. Was I really wrong?

I was sure God was angry with me too! I exaggerated every Scripture passage, every sermon, every lecture. Every time I heard anything about purity I felt like a failure and was so desperate. My view of God, especially as a loving Father, was distorted by my perception of my earthly father. Would God ever get even with me? Could I ever attain and maintain a position of forgiveness and peace? I frequently found myself responding to altar calls to rededicate my life to Jesus Christ. I really wondered if I had committed the unpardonable sin and was doomed forever! My goals soon became pleasing God and people by perfection and service.

Work was something so easy for me to be buried in and that started in early adolescence. I cannot deny that I enjoyed work, and still do. After all, I felt more comfortable in the world of grownups. And I enjoyed the income. I thought money could buy me almost any relationship I wanted. Even though I missed the beach parties and fun with my peers, it was so much easier to escape my loneliness and fear of ridicule by simply working. I could use work as an excuse to miss functions where I thought I might feel uncomfortable. In my late teens, I entered the world of nursing to serve God and escape relationships, a kind of self-punishment. It's true I was challenged by nursing, but I also had unhealthy motivations—I couldn't stand to fail!

It was hard for me to see how the sexual abuse had permeated every area of my life. As long as I could escape its memory, things seemed liveable. As long as nothing attacked my defenses of working and serving God, I lived what others would term a normal Christian life. But things were really out of balance physically, emotionally, socially, spiritually. It became harder and harder for me to try to maintain balance with each new day, week, month and year. The stress was taking its toll.

As part of the balancing act, I worked to keep my past a secret from everyone. "Maybe, just maybe, if people don't know about my past, I will have a chance to be accepted for myself." My thinking was fueled by inner fear. And then a time bomb inside me would explode. My own actions would give me away. I would then use my history of abuse to excuse my behavior and to escape the disapproval of others. Then I wanted pity. It was as if I constantly had to run to avoid some known or unknown source which might detonate the bomb inside of me, shattering my world.

Running to Missions
My running and searching meant frequent change, including a career change. As a little girl, I was so moved by missionary presentations that I had dreamed of the day when I would become a medical mis-

sionary. Then I would remember my secret and think, "I'm dirty. God wouldn't want me as a missionary." But I longed to serve God and please him! Becoming a foreign missionary seemed like the ultimate achievement in the Christian life.

These inner dreams led me to Bible school, short-term missionary service, nursing in a low-income area, and home missions with a national women's organization. I thought that surely if I did my job well, after all these years, God would be lenient with me when he viewed my past.

Being a career missionary had many benefits. It gave me the opportunity to grow and develop in new areas and get to know so many people and families who seemed to have great relationships with each other and with God. I loved my time as a missionary, yet at the same time I had periods of doubt. As far as I was concerned, I was giving beyond the call of duty. Many people respected me and turned to me for spiritual leadership. It was easy for me to share the salvation story of Jesus Christ, never doubting its authenticity. But deep inside I frequently thought that my life was a farce, that the gospel was meant for other people, not for me.

My inner struggles surfaced as perfectionism, authority problems with my leaders and abruptness in peer relationships. Despite (or through) the many struggles, God taught me lessons about balanced living and what healthy family life could be. I'm thankful I can say God was still able to use my life, broken as it was.

I came to believe my struggles were normal in life, especially for a Christian, and I wasn't to talk about them for fear of scaring new Christians and non-Christians away from the kingdom. But the inner pressure became too great for me. Though I would have far rather stayed in the known struggle than turn to the unknown future, I began to believe my life was jeopardizing the lives of others. I realized I would have to leave missionary service. My new worry was "I've been out of nursing so long, who would hire me?" I spent days seriously considering ways I could successfully end my life, but I didn't want to hurt those I loved and cared about.

Time for Another Change

Though I felt like a failure for leaving my life as a missionary, I began to have a sense of excitement that perhaps God had something else in mind for me, new lessons for me to learn. Because I didn't want to return to nursing, I thought that I would need to go back to school to learn some new skills. I had decided my initial choice of nursing was based on the fear that I had to earn acceptance from God and others. I didn't want to act out of fear anymore. So I stepped out to make a vocational change.

I visited three colleges, applied to each and waited to see if I got accepted. I'll never forget my first visit to the college I finally attended. I sat in my car and cried for almost thirty minutes because I was too self-conscious to enter the campus dining room. But once I took the initial step, I knew God had something special in store for me and I could go forward. That feeling was confirmed when all three schools accepted me. I had a successful academic career in psychology.

That was several years ago and over thirty years since I had first talked about my sexual abuse. These past few years have been God's time for deep inner-healing in my life. It has also been a time to gain skills I avoided learning in the normal process of growing up.

This doesn't mean God has not been healing me all along. He kept me from ending my life, especially during times of deep despondency and depression. He helped me maintain my sanity. But in the past, I had only allowed God to patch the surface wounds because I was unwilling to dwell much on my painful past or remind God about it, as if he needed reminding. But as I was willing to expose the wounds, give God the ugliness of the past and forgive my abusers, big changes took place. Though the process put me through almost unbearable pain, God was able to accomplish the deep healing I needed.

For the first time I realized I was the victim of my sexual abuse. The crime had been against me! I was not responsible or guilty! That put the truth of God's forgiveness into perspective. My constant asking God for forgiveness had been futile because I *did not need forgiveness.* Satan had tricked me into false guilt.

As I was able to understand my position as victim, I could thank God for what he wanted to teach me about himself. One evening as I sat on my bed praying, the deep recesses of my life seemed to be pushing out all the anger, pain and hate I had denied or kept hidden for years. For the first time, I knew a new dimension of God's grace, peace, mercy, gentleness and forgiveness as I was able to forgive my abusers. What a replacement for all my anger, doubt, impatience, perfectionism, self-blame and judgmental spirit. I no longer had to be in bondage to my abuse! What a release!

The patterns engraved in my life physically, emotionally, mentally and spiritually for more than forty years have not magically disappeared. But I no longer feel the abuse eating away like a cancer in my life. Life seems so fresh and meaningful! I was abused but never abandoned!

No More Secrets

My story is true. I chose to reveal my identity because you need to know who I am and how common my story is. I wish I *could* tell you that my story is unusual. I suppose in one way it is: it's no longer a secret! Thousands of men, women, boys and girls from every walk of life could tell you a similar story, some far more painful and horrendous.

I can understand the distress of those readers who have lived a similar story. You may fear disclosing your secret. You may be experiencing the pain of guilt, low self-esteem, distortion of spiritual concepts and loss of trust. It may seem easier to continue alone in your self-destructive patterns, rather than face the work involved in healing. I've written to assure you there is hope!

I have included a special section at the back of the book with questions to help victims of abuse respond to this book and deal with the issues of abuse in their own lives. There is also a resource section to help you find more books which will help you deal with the key issues from your own life that you become aware of.

Some of my readers may be angry at those involved in my story. Anger is a normal reaction to abuse. Some readers may be annoyed that I have "rehashed" my story and not forgotten it, even though I claim to have forgiven. I've known others who were angry with me for the opposite—forgiving my father when God clearly hates sin. Readers may direct their anger at my father and the abusers. The police, legal system, other agencies and my mother may be other targets of anger.

Yes, it's maddening to know that such a story is a reality. It is maddening to know that part of my life has been limited or distorted because I was victimized. But a far greater emotion comes to me when I consider the others involved in my story who never received help, who may still be suffering. Or worse yet, may still be abusing others. They, too, need hope and help.

Besides being a normal reaction, anger is a positive emotion when it is used as God intended it—as a motivator to godly action. As you continue to read this book, I hope you will obtain a greater understanding of the "whys" behind abuse and turn your anger into positive action.

Anger isn't the only emotion my story arouses. As you read my story, you may feel pain, sadness, revulsion or a series of other responses. But I did not share my story merely to arouse your emotions. Rather I want to draw your attention to the fact that sexual abuse occurs even within the evangelical community. Unless it is properly treated, it can haunt and cripple a Christian for years.

The place to start treating abuse is in believing that abuse exists. One story may be difficult to believe, let alone all the impersonal statistics in this book. But disbelief that sexual abuse occurs is a major reason it continues. Abuse will not go away if we ignore it; it will only get worse. Disbelief allows the abuser to continue the abuse. Disbelief makes the victim out to be a liar. Fortunately, media attention and other educational efforts are breaking down society's denial of the problem. But Satan still has a foothold—in the evangelical community. Christians believe that sexual abuse exists, but not in their own church congregations. That disbelief allows abuse to spread like an underground fire.

When we admit abuse exists, there is hope and help available for both the abused and abuser! But to understand, we need to look deeply into the issue of sexual abuse. We need to understand what it is, why it has been kept secret, how it has affected our society, how to recognize it and how we can be a part of the solution. I hope this book will help you to understand and act.

—2—

What Is Sexual Abuse?

Four-year-old Misty was beaten and raped as she took a shortcut through a park on her way home one day. Between blows, her attacker explained that he was doing this for her own good. He forced her to say she agreed. Misty's eyes were swollen shut from the bruising by the time she arrived in the emergency room; she had nearly choked to death on semen. It was not expected that Misty would live, but she did.

Thirty years later the incident came back to her—and along with it her only memories of early childhood. She even remembered who had raped her, a pillar of the community who had only recently died. When Misty questioned her mother about the event, her mother denied the incident ever happened. But Misty knew that afternoon thirty years before had affected her life. She would spend many more years defining her experience and understanding its ramifications.

Though Misty has spent many painful hours trying to come to terms with her sexual abuse, outsiders might find her abuse "easier to define" than a more common type—when a seemingly loving father oversteps the line between fatherly closeness and uncontrolled sexual aggression. With differences in cultural, moral and ethical training, the line between sexual health and abuse becomes distorted.

Defining Abuse

Each state has its own legal definition of abuse. In general, child abuse is a nonaccidental injury or pattern of injuries to a child. These include physical injury or abuse, neglect, sexual abuse and emotional abuse.[1]

Severe beating, burns, broken bones or bites are a few examples of nonaccidental injury to a child which would be considered physical abuse. Neglect is "a failure to provide a child with the basic necessities of life: food, clothing, shelter, and medical care."[2] It may mean refusing prescribed medicine to a sick child or warm clothing and shoes for winter. What may appear as neglect in one area of the country may be religious belief or socially acceptable in other parts.

Emotional abuse is much harder to detect or define. It is "excessive, aggressive, or unreasonable parental behavior on the child to perform above his capabilities."[3] This would include extreme belittling, verbal attacks or teasing. But what about ignoring the emotional needs of the child, or offering no verbal communication? The subtle forms of emotional abuse are not easy to detect. Only when flagrant cases appear, such as locking children in rooms, is legal action taken. Unfortunately the effects may not be seen for years.

Is sexual abuse a criminal, social, psychological or spiritual problem? Its definition varies according to your viewpoint. Even the experts struggle with such decisions. The National Health Center on

Child Abuse and Neglect has adapted the following definition of child sexual abuse:

> Contacts or interactions between a child and an adult when the child is being used for the sexual stimulation of the perpetrator or another person. Sexual abuse may also be committed by a person under the age of 18 when that person is either significantly older than the victim or when the perpetrator is in a position of power or control over another child.[4]

Although this is a good working definition, it is limited in its scope. For instance, it deals only with contact between adult and child, without addressing child-with-child contact. And it fails to define the legal ages of a "child" and an "adult." Indeed, each state differs on the point. Some legal definitions limit criminal abuse to parties responsible for the child's care, sometimes even to immediate family members or a guardian's paramour. But what about non-family members? And how does one define sexual gratification?

Where is the line between viewing a child, fondling and intercourse? Are they all sexual abuse? And what about verbal sexual abuse, forcing a child to view another's nakedness or pornographic material or exposing a child to adults engaged in the sex act—how do these fit into the definition?

Out of necessity, each state has had to define sexual abuse in conjunction with its mandatory reporting laws for abused and neglected children. State services such as the Department of Children and Family Services can offer specific information for your state. These laws depend on various definitions, including age of abused or abuser, what constitutes abuse, type of abuse and who is mandated to report such abuse.

In most, but not all, states it is now mandatory for all professionals, including ministers, dentists, teachers, doctors and nurses to report suspected child abuse and sexual abuse to the proper authorities. For this reason, if for no other, it is important that persons working with children know the state and federal child abuse laws . . . before they are called upon to help enforce them.

Types of Sexual Abuse

It will be helpful to know how sexual abuses are classified and understand a little about the different forms of abuse within those classifications. Sexual abuse is often divided into two classifications—touching and nontouching. Nontouching abuse includes verbal abuse, obscene phone calls, watching the sex act performed by others, exhibitionism, voyeurism and viewing pornography. These may or may not be connected with or lead to touching types of abuse.

At first glance, verbal abuse may seem harmless. But for a young child or adolescent, sexual harassment is very demeaning. Although the emotional impact of verbal abuse is a primary concern, the effects can be even more far-reaching—avoidance of normal growth and development. Verbal abuse can also take the form of coaxing a very young child to be sexually precocious. Early sexual prompting may lead to overt sexual involvement.

For instance, because obscene phone calls are often attributed to sick, demented persons or youth who are just "passing through a stage," the calls themselves are somehow assumed to be harmless. The person receiving the calls is told, "Blow a whistle in his ear" or "Hang up on them and they will stop." But to children, these calls can be frightening. If the calls are not talked about with parents who take them seriously and deal with the child's questions and reactions, a child may seek information from sources that don't have the child's best interests in mind.

Often parents consider an infant too young to be affected if intercourse is performed within the baby's viewing or hearing range. However, the National Committee for Prevention of Child Abuse states that "letting down the bars of privacy so that the child watches or hears an act of sexual intercourse" is a type of sexual mistreatment.[5] This is a controversial area, but many psychoanalysts have provided important evidence which supports this conclusion.[6]

Being exposed to unusual sexual behavior may result in vulnerability.[7] Watching the sex act or hearing the sounds that can accompany passionate lovemaking may bring fear to an infant or young child. The child may also see it as a fun game they want to play. Thus, if that same child is approached sexually by an older person, the child may be more ready to cooperate or else be fearful of physical harm. It could also lead to sexual repression or premature sexual activity.[8]

During her high-school years, Leslie was flashed by an older man who was a stranger to her. She told her parents, but they considered it of little concern. When he continued to show up in the places she frequented, repeating the exhibition, they took action, but it was not enough to stop the incidents. She went away to college, but when she returned home on breaks, he would flash her. This continued into Leslie's college years, affecting her in many ways. When she had difficulties relating to her boyfriend, the young man gently discovered the cause and went to the police. Only then did the harassment stop.

Because children and youth don't automatically get over encounters with exhibitionists or the fear of being followed, these abuses need to be taken seriously. This includes the careless handling of pornographic material, which may cause sexually curious children to practice voyeurism—looking at the sexual organs of others for pleasure. The guilt they may feel later needs to be dealt with, not dismissed.

An elderly woman told me of a renter who lived with her family when she was a young child. One day while she was undressing in her upstairs room, she discovered the man peering at her through a heating duct. As she told the story, she could vividly describe the dress she was wearing that day because the experience was so traumatic. Voyeurism can leave its victim feeling totally unprotected. One look *can* do lasting harm.

"Touching" sexual abuse includes fondling, modeling for pornography, prostitution, rape, rape with brutality and murder, and bestiality. The most common types of touching abuse—fondling, oral sex and intercourse—will be explored thoroughly in later chapters. These forms of abuse may be forced on a child separately or together. One may precede another as preparation for further abuse.

Pornography is being considered as one of the major areas of child abuse in our country today. It may be that nontouching abuse (subjecting a child to viewing pornographic materials) or touching abuse (when the child is personally photographed) is preparation for overt sexual activity). The availability of pornographic literature featuring children vividly points out that children are being sexually exploited in every manner possible. The estimate that there are 600,000 child prostitutes remains shocking but does not seem unbelievable.[9]

Rape with brutality or murder may or may not be the result of a one-time sexual involvement between adult and child. Stories of mass homosexual murders sometimes indicate repeated sexual involvement prior to the murder. The sadistic sexual practices and ritualistic sacrifices of babies by cults and others have been exposed as grim reality, not just the lurid subject matter of horror fiction. Though it is equally unimaginable, bestiality, or forcing children to have intercourse with animals, does occur in American society. Because such events are so deplorable, it may seem easier to shut them out of our thoughts as though they never occurred.

Who Is the Abuser?

At one time, sexual abuse was thought to occur most often between total strangers, as in Misty's case mentioned earlier. This idea may have gained acceptance based on the wishful thinking—it was easier for us to accuse a stranger of abuse and to hope a child would forget such abuse.

But once the belief was challenged, an overwhelming number of studies have exposed it for the myth it is. Now the grim facts are acknowledged: over eighty-five per cent of sexual abuse is committed by someone the child knows, loves and trusts. Most often the person who exploits a child is in a legitimate power position over the child.[10] More than fifty per cent of reported cases list parents, parent substitutes and relatives as being responsible for abuse.[11] In most cases, what is labeled *sexual abuse* is really incest.

Incest is sexual abuse between relatives. But in today's changing family, it is difficult to define who is related. Is it considered incest if a mother's live-in boyfriend exposes himself to the woman's daughter? Is it incest if a young boy fondles his stepsister?

We can begin to understand the confusion in definitions—and the many loopholes in application of the laws. The difficulties in defining *incest* have led to inconsistent statistics about its prevalence. Much statistical data has been published recently, yet the studies rarely include a definition of what was meant by the words *incest* or *sexual abuse*. For instance, in one survey sexual abuse may include any touching or viewing of sexual organs. In another, sexual abuse may be limited only to vaginal penetration. When faced with the many conflicting statistics, the public may not believe that sexual abuse is a major problem. How can we believe the statistics? They seem so unreliable.

Statistical Overview

It will be worthwhile for us to take a look at some of the statistics. Even though we do not have the definitions and other factual materials that would help us compare statistic with statistic at our fingertips, an overview of the findings clearly points out the prevalence and seriousness of sexual abuse today. Documentation of sexual abuse is done basically in two ways: (1) incident studies attempting to estimate the number of new cases in a given period and (2) prevalence studies trying to estimate the proportion of the population having experienced sexual abuse during childhood.[12]

For more than forty years, major studies have shown that sexual abuse of children in America has reached nearly a quarter of the population. In 1940 C. Landis found that twenty-three per cent of middle-class hospital patients and controls had been sexually abused before puberty. Kinsey found twenty-four per cent of 4,441 white, middle-class people in 1953 had been sexually abused before puberty. In 1965 Gagnon studied twelve hundred white, middle-class people to find that twenty-eight per cent had been abused before puberty. In 1978 Finkelhor questioned 530 college students. Over nineteen per cent had been abused by an adult, with seventeen per cent of the abuse occurring before puberty.[13] The latest projections, based on hard data, estimate that in 1985 twenty-four per cent (that is, 113,000) of children in the U.S. and its territories had been abused.[14]

While the number of adults admitting abuse in retrospect has remained relatively constant, the number of reported incidents has risen dramatically in recent years. Between 1976 and 1982 reports of all forms of child abuse doubled in the U.S. to more than 1.6 million. Sexual abuse reports also doubled.[15] And reports of sexual maltreatment increased fifty-four per cent between 1983 and 1984.[16]

This can be attributed to at least two factors—the trend in recent years to encourage children to speak up about sexual abuse and the trend for guardians and professionals to report the information to proper authorities. In years past, the norm was silence and inaction. Of forty women with incest histories studied by Herman, 57.5 per cent did not tell their secret at home as a child. Of those who told, mean duration of the abuse was 3.8 years. Over ninety-two per cent had no agency intervention.[17]

It may be that the number of people reporting past abuses will rise as well. The recent media exposure of sexual abuse has helped many adults to release the memory of past abuse. Others are remembering sexual abuse only after years of professional psychological help, an option that is gaining more acceptance year by year. If we were to combine the statistics of those who know they were sexually abused as children with estimates of those abused without remembering it because the trauma was too great, we would find even more alarming numbers.

Females have been reported as being at the greatest risk. But as more studies are conducted, it is becoming obvious that many males have also been abuse victims. A study among more than nine hundred San Francisco women suggests that in this country 160,000 women per million will be victims of incestuous abuse before they reach the age of eighteen.[18] In a retrospective study of 266 male college students, over eight per cent reported childhood sexual abuse. The mean age at the time of abuse was 11.2. In eighty-four per cent of the cases the aggressor was male.[19] It is important to keep in mind that the findings indicate that male sexual abuse is greatly under-reported.[20]

It would be easy to believe that these boys and girls do not come from Christian homes. Perhaps your reaction is, "Look what's happening to society! How sinful! If people would only turn to God, abuse would never occur!"

I wish I could agree. Unfortunately, sexual abuse of children is not just "out there" or in another culture. It is in our American cities, in our home towns and within the church community.

Sexual Abuse in the Christian Community

Until I was almost forty, I was unaware of the widespread problem of sexual abuse even though it had been a major part of my formative years. When I discovered that sexual abuse was not unique to my life, I decided I must become better informed. Little did I know that I could ever find freedom from the effects of the abuse that had bound me in some fashion throughout my life.

As I began reading about sexual abuse, I became angered at the accusations made at the evangelical community, blaming it for causing or sanctioning sexual abuse.[21] Then there were also remarks from within the evangelical community, like "It's not really a problem, is it?" or "It doesn't happen within the church community."

These responses produced mixed feelings within me. I felt weird, strange. If those making the comments only knew of my case, they would have to believe that sexual abuse touched Christians ... or perhaps they would simply doubt my Christianity.

The result of my anger and unrest was the challenge needed to find

out more information about sexual abuse within the evangelical community. I already knew several victims of abuse. These were Christians abused by men who claimed to be Christians—some, leaders
within the evangelical community.

I found no published studies of correlation between sexual abuse
and concept of God. There were also no published studies of the
incidence of sexual abuse and incest among Christians. The only information I came across was surveys which used general questions
about what religion persons were reared in, whether they had a religious preference or whether they were religious.

I then designed and conducted a study within an educational setting to determine the extent to which sexual abuse exists among
Christians and what effect it has had on their concept of God. Even
though the study was limited to a survey of the female students in
a midwestern Christian liberal arts college, the information gained is
worth consideration.

Sexual abuse was defined on the questionnaire as contacts or interactions between a child under the age of eighteen and any other
person when the child was used as an object of gratification for the
other person's sexual needs or desires without the child's consent.
Incest was defined as sexual abuse in the family satellite.

Before beginning the survey, I hypothesized that the rate of sexual
abuse among female Christians would be different than that of the
general population. (Twenty-five per cent are abused.) I predicted that
incest for female Christians would be higher than the general population estimate, suggesting a figure of twenty-six per cent.[22]

A total of 247 female students at a Christian liberal arts college
were asked to participate in the study. Questionnaires, with an ex-
planatory letter and a contact for helpful information after the study,
were personally addressed to every female student reachable by campus mail. The students were instructed to complete the questionnaires
and return them to a designated location anonymously.

Thirty-eight per cent of the questionnaires were returned, or 93 of the 247 distributed. Statistics were compared to the entire 247 female students to prevent any preference for only the returned questionnaires.

Forty-eight students, or nineteen per cent of all female students, reported sexual abuse of some type before the age of eighteen. Incest was reported by thirteen, or five per cent, of all female students. Of the forty-eight students abused, only twenty-one per cent were abused by unknown assailants. Five reported abuse by more than one person.

The following were listed as abusers: father, brother, uncle, cousin, grandfather, boyfriend or fiance, adult leader, friend of the family, neighbor, boss and family physician. A placement home was the scene of one abuse. A grandfather was reportedly abusing each granddaughter. And in another case the abuse was committed by a father who was a minister.

Of those questioned, thirty-six told another person, but some only told in adulthood. Only eleven said that something was done after reporting the abuse. Some reported only part of what happened at the time. Others were able to report and resolve abuse through therapy.

A daughter of missionaries reported an abuse experience to her parents. She was told the abuse was the price she had to pay to be in "his (God's) service." A hickey was discovered on the neck of one victim by a teacher, but nothing was done. A grandmother was told in one case, and she responded by washing the girl's mouth out with soap.

Also presented on the questionnaires were statements about concept of God. Of the abused, thirty-two had changed their concept of God. More abused than non-abused persons had no distinct feelings about God at the time of becoming Christians.

The results of the study show that sexual abuse among female students at one Christian liberal arts college is less than the national average, but it is still high—nearly one in five. Incest for this group was significantly higher than the average population estimates.

I realize that this study is a select sampling, but it shows that sexual abuse does occur to females within the evangelical community. It also demonstrates that sexual abusers are found within the religious community.

No matter which way the statistics are considered, even one case is significant. If sexual abuse can happen to forty-eight Christians who answered my survey, it can happen to others. If the blow comes from one minister, one adult leader or one family physician—and if it strikes one missionary kid—it can affect others. More studies need to be performed and the Christian community needs to do something about the sexual abuse problem.

Of what value then are statistics? Yes, they show that abuse occurs. And that it does happen to some Christians. But how should it affect other Christians? We can take the statistics and apply them to our own settings. In a group of four friends, one may have been abused. In a school or church classroom or Bible study of twenty, five may be victims of abuse. In a church of two hundred, fifty may be victims of abuse. In a workplace of fifty, twelve may have been abused. Five hundred individuals may be direct victims of sexual abuse in a small community of two thousand. If you attend a family reunion of one hundred close relatives, twenty-five could be sexual abuse victims. Alarming!

Even if sexual abuse has not happened to you, it is certain that you will come in contact with those who have been struck by this tragedy. Even if the person is not in your family or church, that person could be among your coworkers, neighbors, business contacts, future in-laws, acquaintances. If not among Christians, perhaps among those who have turned from God because of abuse. You can learn how to help bind up the wounds abuse has caused.

Scapegoats
for
Abuse

*C*hapter two gave evidence that abuse is a real problem, even in Christian circles. For the adult who has experienced childhood sexual abuse—and most likely has kept the abuse a secret, there is a sense of relief in realizing that others have endured the same agony. "I'm not so weird after all! Someone else knows how I feel." Yet not everyone is willing to hear, let alone believe, the grim reality. The same statistics that comfort can confront. This leads to some amazing responses:

"I think it's a media gimmick. It will probably come and go like other fads."

"I've never known anyone who has been abused. If it were really a problem, I would have heard about it earlier in my lifetime."

"I've never seen a clearcut case of incest in all my years as a counselor. It's not really the problem they say it is!"

"That's an awful subject. How can you work with that kind of
person?"

Horror, revulsion, disbelief! Even in the face of a sea of statistics,
some people refuse to face the truth.

When an abuse victim hears comments like these, she may be
shamed into silence once again.* Such comments can diminish any
hope the victim senses. No wonder those writing about sexual abuse
of children have given their books titles like *The Best Kept Secret,
Conspiracy of Silence, A Silence to Be Broken, The Last Taboo* and
Hidden Victims.

Historically, responses to the problem of sexual abuse have not
always been in the victim's best interests. Victims have had to face
distortion of the data, denial of abuse's existence, distraction from the
issue or designation of a scapegoat. Let's take a look at some old
responses and consider how we often use the same coping devices
today in response to sexual abuse.

Distortion and Denial

Freud has become a well-known example of the problems of distortion
and denial in response to sexual abuse. Sigmund Freud is revered for
his work with the emotionally disturbed in the late 1800s. Much of
his analysis was of hysterical women. A detective of sorts, Freud
searched for the cause underlying the hysteria and in many cases
sexual seduction was reported. He told his professional colleagues in
1896 that childhood sexual trauma was the cause of *every* case of
hysteria in *Aetiology of Hysteria* and *Studies on Hysteria.*[1]

---

*Since most abusers are male and most victims female, I have chosen to use masculine
pronouns in reference to abusers and feminine pronouns when talking about the
abused. This does not mean that these statements are necessarily limited to male or
female. You would be able, in most instances, to apply the same information to female
abusers and male victims.

But the personal disclosure of sexual abuse by patients was not Freud's only evidence. Masson and others doing research on Freud have studied his personal papers in depth and exposed other data. Freud had in his possession books detailing childhood sexual abuse which he said verified his theory. Also, Freud himself witnessed autopsies of children who had been sexually abused.[2]

Freud's theory evidently was a shocking revelation to his colleagues. He supposedly was encouraged to reconsider his findings by other professionals.[3] Freud admitted later that his material was "still scanty" and that he "overestimated the frequency" of sexual seduction in childhood.[4] As Freud's psychoanalytic work continued, he stated that the sexual activity had been with older children, mothers or nurses during bodily hygiene.[5]

In the process of trying to discover the cause of hysteria in women, Freud tried to establish insight into the nature of infantile wish fantasies, or Oedipus complex.[6] Using his theory in treating hysterical women, Freud made the following conclusions. First, they showed abnormal desire for obtaining sexual pleasure. Second, they had a pathological tendency to lie and exaggerate, especially about sexual allegations, and had difficulty retelling events. Third, they had a predisposition to hysteria. And fourth, the stories were only fantasies used to cover up typical childhood desires, or an Oedipus complex and autoerotic sexual activity.[7] There is also some belief that later in his practice of psychoanalysis, Freud further changed his theory on the significance of sexual trauma in the cause of emotional disturbance.[8]

We will never really know the truth about Freud's discoveries and beliefs as he is no longer alive to answer questions or defend himself against various charges. When listening to accusations, we need to consider that Freud worked with only a few patients a century ago. Problems of translation, a changing vernacular and his use of technical language should also be taken into account.

Today, the problem of denial continues as people who have been sexually abused are often treated as hysterical due to the changing and wide range of emotions they display. Their stories are written off as hallucinations, dreams or exaggerations. When the victim blocks all or part of the incident from her mind, it is labeled amnesia or a hysterical reaction. When the person at this stage is not believed, a further hysterical reaction can occur.

Another form of denial may be to assume that a child is telling tales to get attention. If this is so, where would a child get such detailed sexual information? We must keep in mind that a child does not have adult sexual fantasies and desires. We do need to consider the emotional constitution of each abuse victim in treatment for healing, but this factor should not be allowed to minimize the trauma of the abuse.

Distraction

Distraction from the issue of sexual abuse may be seen in the Kinsey studies. In 1953 Kinsey became a household word when he reported the results of extensive surveys. One was personal interviews with over four thousand young, White, predominately middle-class, urban, educated women. Twenty-four per cent of the women reported childhood sexual encounters to Kinsey's investigative team. Of these, eighty per cent expressed being frightened and upset by the experience.[9]

An exhaustive survey was also conducted with five thousand men. No numerical report was made on the sexual contacts between boys and adults, but statistics did indicate that most of the contacts were homosexual.[10]

Kinsey said publicly that a child should not be upset by such sexual approaches. But we do not know what he used as a working definition of "childhood sexual encounters." If the child was upset, he believed that blame should be placed on prudish parents or teachers who, in response to the reported approach, caused the child to become hysterical. He further explained that cultural conditioning would cause a child to be upset with genital fondling.[11]

Kinsey was a pioneer in the field of human sexuality. The purpose of his surveys was not to study incest. His studies made public the existence of sexual encounters between adults and children. We do not know that this was a purposeful distraction. It could be unfair to compare his general surveys to specific surveys of others. Each type of survey uses a different set of questions and populus. The surveyor chooses the emphasis.

It is interesting to note that in 1955, only two years after Kinsey's study, S. Kirson Weinburg published *Incest Behavior*. This study was based on 203 cases of sexual abuse known to agencies in the Chicago area. There was reportedly no public response of any kind to the study.[12]

Thus, sexual abuse is at times seen only as being a minor part of other problems. For instance, when treating individuals for problems such as substance abuse, eating disorders, suicide attempts, running away or prostitution, the focus of the treatment is not on the underlying fact of the abuse, but on these resulting actions. This distraction from the abuse may temporarily provide an end to such actions, but not heal the core problem of abuse.

Designation of a Scapegoat

It has seemed so easy for some to accuse Freud and Kinsey of distortion, denial or distraction from the issue of sexual abuse. Yet, these are only two examples of accusations. Focusing blame on them can make us guilty of the same accusations. It is in fact designating a scapegoat, an easy answer to a complex problem. It is an intellectual way of avoiding an emotionally laden problem.

A closer look at mythology, storybooks, nursery rhymes, history books and the Bible reveals that sexual abuse has existed in many forms for years. Some of these sources, used to teach moral and social principles, clearly devalue children and treat them as property.

Consider the Frog King, the tale of a young princess who lost her ball in the water. The frog promises to retrieve the ball in exchange for her love, food from her little plate and sleep on her little bed. At first the princess considers this nonsense and agrees to the frog's demands. Later the nasty frog appears at the door of the princess, reminding her of the promise. The king makes his daughter keep her promise. Then, the frog turns into a prince. The two live happily ever after.[13]

In Rumpelstiltskin the miller's daughter promises the funny little man her first-born child in exhange for spinning gold out of straw. The dwarf returns after the child is born. Although the spell was broken and the promise not fulfilled, a young child was used as trade.[14]

In another tale, Bearskin was promised his choice of an old man's daughters. They were all repelled by the appearance of the man. The betrothed dressed in black and was mocked and teased by her sisters. Bearskin changed from his beastly appearance into a handsome lover when he returned for his betrothed.[15]

There are many other tales which could be used as examples. It is not unusual to see children or young females bargained off or promised in marriage. The wording is not so bold, but the implications are powerful.

Society has not chosen to face the issue openly. Scapegoating seems to be a present-day reaction to sexual abuse. Sometimes alcohol or drug abuse is seen as the primary culprit. There are cases in which alcoholism has been used to cover up the guilt of abuse. Substance abuse has been used by some sexual abusers as an excuse for their behavior.

Other factors have been thought to be more widespread sources of the problem. Consider the following examples. Florence Rush has become a much-quoted authority on sexual abuse. She makes an accusation that the Bible and the Talmud encourage sex between little girls and men.[16] She takes extensive steps to expose details.

In her book *The Best Kept Secret,* Rush unfortunately fails to distinguish between the Talmud, the Bible, the Koran, witchcraft and other sources, but frequently lumps them together in her accusations. The Talmud gives explicit ages for marriage or sexual transactions with very young children. Scripture does talk of sexual abuse, giving examples. But nowhere does Scripture encourage sex with very little girls in marriage, concubinage and slavery as stated by Rush. Rush incorrectly assigns to the Talmudic commentary and tradition the same weight of authority as the Bible.

It would be an easy mistake for a person who did not see two distinct forces at work in the Jewish religion to make: God (the author of inspired Scripture) and men (who interpreted Scripture in the rabbinic writings of traditional Judaism). Six times in the Sermon on the Mount Jesus himself confronted the same issue of failure to distinguish between the tradition of the rabbis and the pure teaching of Scripture.

Rush further accuses the Old Testament Scriptures of teaching that women are property, and therefore vulnerable to sexual exploitation. She makes this accusation based on the command in which God seems to categorize a man's wife with his ox and house. She sees the female as sexual property and all heterosexual relationships as financial transactions.

Says Rush: "Marriage was the purchase of a daughter from her father, prostitution was a selling and reselling of a female by her mother for sexual service, and rape was the theft of a girl's virginity which could be compensated for by payment to her father. Where the Bible was vague regarding the age of females in these transactions, the Talmud was explicit."[17]

The assumption that wives must be "property" because they are mentioned in the same sentence with oxen does not follow logically. In addition, the last sentence unfairly implies guilt where none exists. The Bible is not "vague." Rather, it is silent, making no statements about required or recommended ages for females to marry. Freedom for individuals to use intelligence in making their decisions is honored.

The Bible does not specify a bride price or dowry as essential or recommended for marriage to be binding. Dowries were part of Hebrew cultural marriage customs. The moral, civil and ceremonial law which was given to Moses should not be confused with Hebrew custom or any other Eastern custom.

These are only two of the many accusations Rush has made about abuse implicating the Bible and Christianity as culprits. It would be wise to sift through such a book, quoted as authority, to differentiate between the Bible, the Talmud, the Koran, the Mishna, mythology, witchcraft and tradition. As we shall see, the Bible does speak out clearly on abuse, giving examples and setting up guidelines for identifying, avoiding and punishing abuses.

Walters also accuses our Judeo-Christian heritage of being responsible for abuse of children:

> The physical and sexual abuse of children does not occur in a cultural vacuum. Rather, America has a long history of treating children as inferiors, as little more than chattel to be done with as the adult caretaker wishes.
>
> The status of children in present-day America has its roots in history, specifically in the Bible. For generations, we have been a people strongly influenced by the Bible. We have tried to pattern our lives after its teachings, and to a large degree this book has influenced our interpersonal relationships, our handling of children, and the status of children in our society. Out of our Judeo-Christian heritage came laws that formalized the biblical status, roles, and relationships, and today attorneys are still struggling with legal problems connected with the abuse of children.[18]

Just because Americans behave in a certain way does not mean that is how God intended them to behave, especially when their behavior clearly contradicts God's commands. And Walters fails to mention the prohibition against incest in Scripture: "No one is to approach any close relative to have sexual relations" (Lev 18:6). It is true that abuse occurs in Christian and Jewish homes, but it also occurs in nonreligious homes, as well as in cults which use a religious cover.

God's clear intention is that sexual intimacy be accompanied by permanent commitment in a one man-one woman relationship. Under this law a man does not have the opportunity for promiscuity without accountability. It is a law that does not permit a "throwaway" mentality toward women. Relationships with women require responsibility and accountability, not exploitation.

The punishment for taking indecent liberties with a young woman under Mosaic law was more severe than most ardent modern proponents of reform would dare suggest to our humanistic American society. There is scarcely a more imaginable deterrent to sexual immorality and abuse than what is described in Deuteronomy 22:25-29.

> But if out in the country a man happens to meet a girl pledged to be married and rapes her, only the man who has done this shall die. Do nothing to the girl; she has committed no sin deserving death....

If laws like this were ever enforced, sexual abuse would scarcely have opportunity to germinate, let alone produce the deplorable harvest it has produced for centuries in our Western culture.

It is important to remember that God gave us biblical principles for our protection and so that we would realize our need for him. Whether our sympathies lie with the abused or the abuser, God's principles are practical.

Christ met the harsh demands of justice when he paid with his life the debt of every offender of God's law. His grace and healing are available for everyone. And the New Testament teaching on church discipline recognizes the full meaning of justice and grace. It has redemptive, restorative purposes as its primary intent. (See Mt 18:15-19; 1 Cor 5:14-21; 2 Cor 2:1-11.)

It would be unfair for you to be left with the idea that Freud, Kinsey, Rush and Walters are the only ones who have distorted, denied, distracted from or designated scapegoats for sexual abuse. That is not my intent. In briefly explaining their writings I hoped to convey that we as humans have great difficulty in dealing squarely with sexual abuse.

The past few years writing this book have been a major struggle

for me. The struggle has not been so much in dealing with the issues
of abuse as wrestling with the responses of others—the ever-present
problems of scapegoating, denial and victimization. Here are just a
few of the remarks I have heard:

"You don't have the right to tell about it"—my brother. (His impli-
cation was that I must have consented since the abuse went on for
so long, and thus the abuse was my fault.)

"There is no need. Incest is such a small thing. Yours is over"—a
missions director.

"How can you write a book? You haven't worked through everything yet"— another victim.

"Letting people know you have been abused will jeopardize your
work with children. You know how parents have preconceived ideas
about people who have been abused"—a psychiatrist. (These preconceived ideas would include expecting inappropriate sexual behavior
from the victim, as well as psychological or social maladjustment.)

Denial and distraction have kept me from doing my part toward
prevention and healing sexual abuse. I have denied my ability to share
the lessons I have learned and the healing I have experienced from
sexual abuse. I challenge you to look at your part in blaming or scapegoating. Please use the energy of your anger to bring about creative
change.

Whether professionals, church leaders or parents, we must look at
the facts: sexual abuse is a present-day problem which must be faced
and confronted. Only in doing so will we be able to bring our sick
society back to God's principles for holy living.

−4−

The Climate
for
Abuse

What better activity for a twelve-year-old than a church youth group!

Steve had lived alone with his mother, Lillian, since his father had left them. Even when his father had been around he wasn't much of a father. He had been physically abusive to both Steve and Lillian. In a way there was more peace with his being gone, but in another way there was a real sense of loss.

Steve, in the bloom of adolescence, was ready for some independence. He wanted to be like his peers. But he still needed his mother's warmth and love, especially since the divorce. However, his mother's quietness resulted in his feeling unwanted. Her sudden outbursts of anger resulted in his feeling guilty. Her despondency and lack of interest in anything other than work led to a feeling of desperation.

Lillian had been unable to respond to many of Steve's emotional needs because she had been so hurt by the divorce that she didn't even trust her own feelings. She enjoyed a quiet home, and Steve's noise often got on her nerves. She wondered whether he understood that she was doing all she could for him. It took all she had just to keep the rent paid and food on the table. What else did he need?

What a relief when Curt took an interest in him! At sixteen, Curt had his own car and part-time job. Lillian was relieved that such a clean-cut guy would take an interest in her son. Instead of bugging her, the two boys could be together. Instead of being alone at home when she worked, Steve would be with Curt. Instead of the bother of Lillian driving Steve places, Curt was more than willing. And much more important, Curt was involved in the local church.

Steve and Curt were like brothers. Their time together seemed healthy and well-spent. Curt would listen to Steve for hours sometimes. Steve actually was able to cry and found that Curt would hold him. Curt really understood! Curt really cared!

Curt had a growing interest in sexual things—as adolescents normally do. Steve was also curious. He was aroused by the pornographic magazines Curt had around. Steve knew that Curt often experienced sexual tension and tried to get relief by masturbating. Steve soon found himself in the same routine of pressure, pleasure, relief and comfort. Then Steve began mutual masturbation with Curt, his role model and nurturer.

As for Lillian, she knew that Steve was masturbating—but didn't all teen-age boys? She was just relieved he had a good friend.

Steve and Curt continued to do everything together. By the time Steve was sixteen, Curt had helped him land a job at the same place he worked. Steve soon had little interest in home or school. All he wanted to do was be with Curt. No one questioned that Curt never dated through his teen years. Everyone thought it was neat that younger boys gravitated to Curt and Steve like little puppy dogs.

And then it hit. The parents of one of the younger boys got suspicious about Curt's little flock. Their son had been very disturbed about unusual sexual activities. He had been forced to tell his parents, after becoming physically ill. The family physician quizzed the parents when medical tests exposed herpes.

The shock was doubled when the police raided Curt's apartment and found Steve, other young boys and all types of sexual paraphernalia. How could so much bad be hidden in all the good?

*   *   *   *   *   *   *   *   *

Ralph and Claire had what most people considered the perfect marriage. They had met and married while still in their teens. Ralph managed to keep his little family together during his time in the military. Even though the years were difficult, Ralph left the military with all the training he needed to be a pilot.

A pilot's salary allowed Ralph, Claire and their children, David and Molly, to build their dream home in the country. Perhaps the excitement of a new home with all the material blessings would make up for the time Ralph was gone from home.

Claire tried to busy herself with activities in the country club, their church and the children's school. But the years of Claire's unsettled childhood, coupled with the years of military moves, took their toll on her. Claire never let anyone too close to her. The country home afforded this privacy.

Ralph spent half his time at home and half in the air. So as time went on, instead of growing closer, Ralph and Claire found their relationship more and more strained. Ralph wanted to make up for lost time when he was home. Claire found herself cold to Ralph's sexual advances. How could he expect her to feel turned on when she was so insecure?

So they focused their energies on their children. Molly got involved in horses. At thirteen she was growing into quite a young lady—and an excellent rider. Ralph didn't seem to mind that David was something of a mama's boy since Molly was so interested in sports.

The horses meant time, money and clothes for Molly. Ralph gave her all she wanted and managed to be home for most of her shows. It wasn't unusual for Ralph to treat Molly to overnight stays in motels after horse shows instead of spending late hours driving home. Claire didn't like the travel and preferred to stay at home with David.

But somehow things just didn't seem right to Claire. Molly knew too much about sex for a young adolescent. Why would she be concerned about birth control information? Why on the one hand did she love her horse shows, but on the other hand appeared so uptight when her father returned home to take her to one?

For some time Claire questioned Ralph about whether he was involved with another woman because his interest in sexual activity with her had all but disappeared. But Ralph denied it.

Molly saw the rift and took her father's side. Molly would do anything to keep her family together. By the time Molly was seventeen, she could hardly stand the arguing between her parents. She couldn't stand David's jealousy of her as favorite. If he only knew the truth. Her father's living at home half the time was better than not at all. What would her mother do if Ralph did not provide financially? And Molly loved all the material things that an intact family provided.

The family was involved in church—at least on Sundays. Molly believed in God and took a strong moral stand. But there were certain things she did not understand. Her father claimed to be a Christian, but his moral standard with her was different from the one taught by her mother and the church.

The situation exploded when Molly became pregnant at seventeen. What was she to do? How could she tell her mother that the baby belonged to her father? Instead, Molly first tested her mother by telling her about "a friend." Her mother's response made it clear that Molly could not tell the truth.

She considered abortion, but did not want to destroy the baby. Suicide was considered, but she thought that would destroy her mother too. Then what would happen to her brother? She decided the only alternative was to run away.

Molly had her baby but never told who the father was. Even though she later returned home to live with her mother, the relationship was not good. Ralph soon deserted his family. Who knew if he was running to another woman or running away from guilt?

The truth of the incestuous relationship only came out as Molly got involved in a single parent's group. She found that she was not the only mother struggling with poor self-esteem. She felt guilty for her strained relationship with her mother and hatred of her father. She was fearful for the safety of her child.

* * * * * * * *

Sunday morning, Sunday night, Wednesday night! Every time the church doors were open, Joe and Mary were there. Mary and Joe were committed to growing in what they thought were the most significant ways—and that meant religiously. Mary constantly poured herself into Bible study, the women's missionary society, choir and community affairs.

Joe also wanted to live out what they had been taught: your priorities were first Jesus, then others and last yourself. Joe spent most of his time at work or at church. It was not unusual for him to be at church meetings three or four times a week. He was always available to help the pastor or the deacons, no matter what was going on at home.

It was only natural for their children, Tom and Sue, to be taken to all the church's activities. Even when they were babes in arms, Joe insisted that Mary keep them in adult church services. Restlessness, tears, sickness—none were cause to change the household's church routine. Tom and Sue were raised to be the perfect children in the perfect Christian home. Sunday school, Bible memory work, family devotions were all ingrained into their young lives. Almost as soon as they began to play with other children, they learned to witness to their friends about God's plan of salvation. Their parents stressed the importance of separation from the worldly things.

As perfect children, both Tom and Sue were potty-trained early. Tom was such a good little boy—really mama's big helper—looking after Sue when Mary took time for personal devotions. Tom and Sue were weaned early from cuddling. From early childhood, their emotional needs became covered up or ignored by Joe and Mary. Despite the fact that their parents denied their need for physical contact, those needs did not disappear.

At first the children could not conceal their emotions. But they quickly learned control in the face of their father's threats of spankings and other disciplinary actions. On the outside this family was seen as "the perfect family." On the inside, the children were scared. Because the parents seemed so perfect, no one thought they had needs. No one stopped to ask questions. Joe and Mary were emotionally isolated from other people. Their religiosity had become quite a front.

If there were Bible studies in their home in the evenings, the children were to be quiet in their rooms. Sue would often cry to sleep at night after being sent to her room. Tom's feeling of responsibility for Sue was strong; he couldn't stand her tears. Tom would slip in bed with Sue to calm her. The physical touch was so comforting to both of them. Sue depended on Tom for cuddling, bathing, dressing. They had a life together that no one else shared.

Through the years the family situation changed. They all became more involved in their activities and deadened to their emotions. Tom and Sue went from innocent comfort to frequent sexual involvement. Sue loved Tom for watching after her. She knew he needed comfort when their father meted out severe discipline or had sudden outbursts of his temper. Sue was there for comfort. Sue had learned that sexual activity was not considered appropriate, but how could she turn her brother away? He pouted or threatened to coerce her into cooperating sexually. In some ways, Sue was relieved to be forced.

Their times together were the only joy they had.

* * * * * * * * *

Why does sexual abuse occur? What kind of situation is conducive to sexual abuse? If there were an easy answer to these questions, perhaps we could have put a stop to the problem by now. Through the years there have been numerous explanations, but no one explanation is adequate. The truth is, the answer will be as complex as the problem. To help set the context for understanding some theories of why abuse occurs, let me say a few words about normal sexual activity for children.

Childhood Sexuality

Children do have a natural sexual curiosity which should not be confused with inappropriate or abnormal sexual behavior. When a three- or four-year-old child views the diaper changing or potty training of a younger sibling, a parent should not hesitate to discuss anatomical differences.

For a child, novelties are often explored by sight and touch. Touching one's body parts is a normal part of exploration and discovery. This is especially prevalent in infancy, young children and adolescents.

Seeking hugs and kisses is natural, and easily mimicked from parental examples. Sitting on dad's lap or strutting around scantily dressed in childhood are some ways of vying for direct attention.

A young boy may try to sneak a look at Mom's, or his teen-age sister's nude body. During high school, comparing size in gym class and watching the bodies of those of the opposite sex as they walk down the hall are results of natural sexual curiosity.

These are to be distinguished from inappropriate sexual behavior for children, such as always walking around without adequate attire, continuous fondling of self or others or excessive desire for caressing and deep kissing.[1] Looking at pornographic material can result from curiosity or peer pressure. (Intent and meaning are different in pornography and art.) But a person who gains sexual gratification from pornography has gone beyond curiosity.[2]

Sexual thoughts and fantasies are also part of human nature. They are a source of present pleasure and planning for the future. They may or may not be accompanied by masturbation. But they become a problem if they become uncontrolled and a detriment to other areas of life.[3]

Theories for Occurrence

With that as background, let's consider possible reasons why abuse occurs.

"It's what the child wants": How can an adult ignore the cute behavior of a young child? A little girl sits on her daddy's lap and begins kissing him the way Mommy does. A little child prances around nude like the models on cable television. A little boy sucks on a friend's ponis or has his sister suck his. Really, a child is asking for sexual attention from an adult. Or so some believe. And if a child asks, then isn't that the cause?[4]

To the theory that a child's behavior causes sexual abuse, there are several responses. First of all, where did that child learn the sexual behavior? It didn't just appear. If from television or literature, who produced the explicit material in the first place? Not children. And if a child does act out, an adult or older child does not have to comply. A child cannot make an adult sexually exploitive. Surely adults have some control over themselves. By size, age and authority they have more power than children. The child's actions do not add up to the cause of sexual abuse.[5]

The compliant child: Another theory focuses on the sexually defenseless, compliant child. This theory proposes that one should not call the sexual involvement *abuse* if the individual does not consider it wrong or if the child willingly complies. This theory assumes that a young child can decide right versus wrong, healthy versus unhealthy, normal versus abnormal.

But children who are reared to embrace wrong, unhealthy, abnormal behavior cannot be expected to instinctively know the truth. How can a child who is reared in an open social setting where sexual activity with anyone, including children, is considered normal think otherwise?

And if their needs, fears and depravations are great enough, many children will comply even if they suspect their actions are wrong. A child may even ask for sexual relationships in order to be included as an acceptable member of the group. When physical or emotional force is placed on a child, a child fears brutality. To avoid further trauma a child will readily comply to giving sexual favors. Such behavior should be blamed on the adult, not the child. An older person or adult should have more power to stop the abuse, even if the child seems to want it.[6]

Social isolation: This is the first of three theories based on the dynamics of the family. The socially isolated family becomes involved in their own little world. They look to each other to meet all their needs. They look to themselves for norms. If sexual activity is within the family, it becomes normal behavior for the children. Instead of social interaction with peers to learn autonomy and intimacy, a teen turns to family. In such a family a child is expected to remain within the network. Any questioning of sexual activity would be considered rebelliousness.[7]

Role confusion: Role confusion occurs when a person allows personal needs to overshadow the normative roles of being the father, mother or child. With role confusion, a father might think, *Why should a man not be fulfilled sexually within his own home?* and then overlook his wife to find a sex partner in his daughter.[8]

It may be that the mother is ill or unable to sexually fulfill her husband. The child may be considered grown up before her time. "What a little mother" sounds like a compliment. But a child expected to take on adult responsibilities, such as tending younger children or running the home, can find herself in the position of lover as well as wife and mother. In some cases a teen-age girl may take more time with her appearance, becoming a sexual rival to her mother. The father becomes a peer to the daughter and begins to regard his wife as his mother. He finds it more comfortable to be mother's little boy because he doesn't have to meet society's standards.

Other times a wife may feel rejected when her husband is abusive, away from home frequently or unable to fulfill her needs. She may turn to her young son for sexual fulfillment. Sometimes in a single-adult home, sexual favors are asked of a child. In none of these cases does a child cause sexual abuse. It is up to the adult to prevent the abuse and find appropriate ways to meet personal needs.[9]

Pressure to keep the family together: In some instances, as in the case of Ralph and Molly, a child may think he or she must comply with sexual abuse to keep a parent from leaving or to protect the family.

This fear of abandonment should not be seen as the root cause of abuse. No child should be the cement to keep a family together. A family exhibits deep-seated needs when a child is led to believe that Daddy will leave or get in trouble, Mommy would get mad or die, or Daddy will do it to the other children if the abuse is made known. A mother who knows of such a situation and does not get help is considered as guilty as the perpetrator.[10]

Sexual addiction, compulsion and deviance in developmental sequence: These theories, which will be discussed in more detail later, suggest that there is a lack of inhibition or adequate developmental training which results in abuse. In other words, an inner component compels a person to abuse as a means of gratification or as a coping mechanism.

Adolescent offender: There are several types of adolescent offenders. Some may fit into the above categories. Others may be more naive experimenters. Group influence, more significant during adolescence, is a factor in causing abuse. The need to impress peers, gain peer approval or acceptance, or win a dare all lend pressure.

The sin nature: There are other theories as to why sexual abuse occurs, but the bottom line is that sexual abuse is a result of the sin nature in people—and one of the most divisive tools used by Satan throughout history. He has capitalized on the embarrassment people feel in order to keep sexual abuse hidden. With it hidden and the guilt of the abuser and false guilt of the abused festering inside the individuals, little can be done to stop abuse or help the abused or abuser.

Satan is the great accuser, the father of lies. He would have us forget that sexual abuse is a sin and crime against the creation of God. If we ignore the sin issue in favor of only the physical, emotional or social issues, its vicious cycle will not be stopped. There must be a balanced view of the issues. We must not lose sight of the fact that God's creation includes all of the physical, emotional, social and spiritual aspects of humanity. All must be considered in the cause of sexual abuse.

Because sexual abuse affects a person physically and emotionally, we must understand that stopping abuse will not make a victim whole—that will take years of healing. Because it is a social issue, until it is well publicized and until the law enforcement and judicial systems are changed by informed citizens, the problem can only grow worse. Because it is a spiritual issue, concerned Christians have the duty of bringing the hope of Christ's redemption to the abused and the abuser.

Contributing Factors in the Home

There is no easy way to describe the family in which sexual abuse occurs. It can and does hit almost every type of family and in many social settings. The three cases at the beginning of this chapter describe overt sexual abuse, but all forms of abuse can occur within the same dynamics.

As we look at the climate of abusive families, we can see some common contributing factors. These are not seen in all families nor do these factors necessarily indicate that sexual abuse is occurring.

Rather, they are typical indicators.

Low self-esteem: Parents with low self-esteem breed children with low self-esteem. Individuals with low self-esteem frequently demean others so that they themselves look and feel better. The success of abuse builds esteem and confidence in the abuser in one sense. In the example of Curt and Steve, they received some emotional reinforcement from having the little band of followers. But perpetrating abuse can at the same time make the abuser defensive and oversensitive to any type of criticism.[11] He develops a false sense of self-esteem.

The children who are being abused may be devastated by the abusive behavior they are forced to submit to. They may look outside of the family for some feeling of worth. At the same time, the attention of a pedophile may provide a sick fulfillment of a child's need to feel special.[12]

Children with low self-esteem may welcome an abuser's attentions. Because children develop at different rates, they are able to accomplish only certain tasks realistically. If unrealistic expectations are placed on a child, the child may reap punishment or little expression of love and acceptance, forcing the child to go to sources outside the home for love and acceptance. That was the situation with Tom and Sue, the brother and sister we considered earlier.[13]

Poor interpersonal relationships: With poor or shallow interpersonal relationships, especially with a spouse, a person may look elsewhere for relationships. Adults may then look to younger children for fulfillment. A misunderstood child may look to a source outside the family who may be a perpetrator.[14]

Lack of normal social and emotional contacts outside the home is much the same experience isolative individuals have. However, some people are involved with groups or activities such as church but do not develop in-depth relationships. Such in-depth relationships or friendships provide communication of needs and someone with whom they can be accountable. Social activity can be a cover-up for what is really happening within an individual or family context.[15]

In families where sexual abuse occurs, secretiveness provides safety for the abuser. Abused and abuser have their own communication system. Unhealthy diads further break down family unity, increasing the climate for sexual abuse.[16]

Emotional overload: Pressures such as a crisis or series of crises can frustrate a family. Such overload of emotions can result in anger or demonstrations of power shown in sexual abuse. An adult may also seek nurture and love expressed in a sexual way from a child.[17]

Special needs: Children with special needs or physical abnormalities find themselves easy prey for an abuser. Such children are seldom able to report any such abuse. Others may consider the abuse as normal treatment from children or adults, or they may come to depend on the "comfort" it brings.[18]

Jill was a mute child from birth. Neither she nor her mother had learned to sign with ease, so she could not tell her mother about the sexual abuse by her uncle. She became distressed as the abuse continued, and her mother became puzzled by her sadness. An acquaintance at church who was signing for services became interested young child. She herself was an adult survivor of incest, just remembering the events during that period of time. She soon suspected Jill was in an abusive situation. She located a detailed signing book of sexual descriptions. Through much time with this special needs child, the abuse was disclosed and the uncle taken to court.

Prolonged absence of the mother or father from the home may also make abuse more likely. Illness or death of a spouse may contribute even further to the climate of abuse unless the sexual and nurturing needs of parents and child are met in appropriate ways.[19]

Need for attention: A further reason for sexual abuse is the need for attention and recognition. A spouse who is not given attention sexually may try to find it in other places.[20] Whether the lack of attention is accidental or on purpose, either may lead to abuse. A child who needs attention and nurturing readily thrives on any attention shown. The child's return to the abuser may be all the recognition the abuser needs.

Substance abuse: Alcoholism or other substance abuse within a setting can also be factors in abuse. It is interesting to note that in the
first two places in the Bible in which incest is mentioned alcohol is
involved (Gen 9:21-27; 19:30-36).[21] In some cases it has been found
that the alcoholism is a cover-up for the guilt of abuse.[22] It would seem
that the drugs dull the pain and bring out base needs. In others it
provides false courage to act on their impulses. Although it is not a
direct cause, it is an indicator of psychosocial dysfunction.[23] Alcoholism has been used as an excuse for sexual abuse, but it is never a
sufficient excuse for abusive behavior. Substances have also been used
in the process of abuse, such as in cases where children have been
drugged and sexually abused in ritualistic manners by groups.

A number of similarities between alcoholic and incestuous families
have been noted:

1. Blurred generational boundaries.
2. Dysfunction between the husband and wife and inadequate parenting.
3. Deterioration of the marital sexual relationship.
4. Inhibitions are short-circuited or muted.
5. Family emotions are muffled and distorted.
6. Denial and "secrets" predominate.
7. Family roles are rigid and unnatural.
8. The family becomes isolated, emotionally and otherwise.
9. The family becomes stuck in its pathological state.
10. Sibling relationships become pathologically disturbed.
11. Either belonging or separateness in the family becomes extreme.
12. Intimacy and trust problems exist.
13. Dependency issues arise.[24]

Inconsistent standards and poor discipline: Survivors of sexual
abuse often tell of growing up in homes where the mother and/or
father are seen as too strict or prudish, perhaps as a result of a
legalistic or fundamentalist background.[25] A parent ruling the household by fear and friction may prevent a child or spouse from reporting

abuse. The actual sexual abuse may be welcomed as a gentle relief from harsh physical trauma.[26]

Other survivors said their parents had I-don't-care attitudes toward discipline which the children later realized to be too lenient. Or they mentioned parents who vacillated between the two ways of handling discipline. Such vacillation is confusing to a child, especially when moral standards are involved. Parents who have conflicting views of sex or who consider sex as dirty may project these views on their own children.[27]

Lack of privacy: Common sleeping arrangements provide no privacy for children or parents. When sexual intimacy is close at hand, it becomes very difficult for children or parents to resist participation in unhealthy sexual activities.[28]

Other factors: Unresolved anger, immature parents, unmet nurturance and other needs, as seen in the situations at the beginning of this chapter, all create climates which may breed abuse.

Every parent has the potential to abuse a child at some time. Most abusive people are considered normal. Relatively few are considered mentally unbalanced.[29] Abuse, no matter what type, can occur in any climate. Usually abuse reflects the way the abuser learned how to cope with inner stress or how to get needs met as he or she was growing up.

As we can see, with no one home climate leading to sexual abuse, it becomes difficult to get to the heart of the problem. The abused, abuser, and whole family system need hope and help to prevent sexual abuse, and to heal the wounds when it has already taken place.

—5—

Characteristics
of
Abusers

---

*I*t takes more than a certain "climate" for sexual abuse to occur. "The devil made me do it" is not an adequate explanation for such behavior. There are common reasons for its occurrence and typical characteristics of individuals who sexually abuse children. Not all people with the following traits are necessarily child abusers or will inevitably become child abusers. Likewise, not all child abusers exhibit all of these characteristics. Nonetheless, it is instructive to see what patterns research has uncovered.

Contributing Personality Factors

Poor parental model: Surveys are now revealing that the abuser or parents of the abused were often abused in childhood. Hank Giarretto, who has worked with abusive families for over fifteen years, has data showing that about ninety-five per cent of the parents of abuse victims were abuse victims themselves.[1] It's not that a person would choose to put his or her own child in an abusive situation. For some, it is the only pattern of living they know. They might consider it normal—or unavoidable—for a child to be sexually abused.[2]

Isolative personalities: There are isolative individuals who think that no one should know about their problems. These people lack any consistent sense of intimate attachment.[3] This is an area where Christians can especially be caught in a cycle of abuse because they believe Christians should live happy, joy-filled lives at any cost. When trouble does come, it is thought that the pain and hurt (losing a job, death of a friend, car accident) should be ignored, kept inside or distorted. Some have had parents or friends who have ignored or ridiculed them for expressing difficulties. Emotions are then vented on children, or their needs are met in inappropriate ways.

Compensation for rejection: Rejection can take many forms: divorce, marriage refusal, parental rejection, sexual rejection or social rejection. When a person is rejected, the natural response is to compensate by finding some form of acceptance since people are created with needs for affiliation and the need to be needed. A person may find himself or herself to be sexually acceptable to minors. Inadequacies with the adult world are thus magnified.[4]

Inability to define role boundaries: It is common for male incest abusers to have difficulty distinguishing the role boundaries of wife and daughter. This can occur in two quite different ways. The first allows his wife to fulfill the role of a mother. He is more comfortable as a "little boy" who does not have to meet normal social or familial expectations. And with wife as mother, it is easier for daughter to become a lover.

The second way role boundaries are confused is by those who find it difficult to understand the role of women at all. Sometimes this is covered up with domineering attitudes by the husband. He lets his wife know that he will accept no deviation from the way he expects the household to be run. The husband may consider her incapable of satisfying him emotionally. Simultaneously, the wife may be emotionally unsupportive or negligent to her husband.

Such a person can be what is called overadequate in which a façade of being a superfather or superhusband covers up an underlying sense of inadequacy. Most people viewing an overadequate parent from the outside would only think he had it all together. But it can create potential for abuse in the home. Whether the parent is dominated by his spouse or dominates his spouse, the abusive parent is inadequate in the parenting role.[5]

Faulty concept of sexuality: Sexual abusers often have only a superficial appreciation of sexuality. Whether married or single, male or female, sexual involvement and gratification is frequently the person's main concern.[6]

A defense against powerlessness: Feelings of powerlessness and lack of control lead to a fear of destruction. Without power, one feels helpless. Without control, one feels like a pawn. It becomes a compulsion to regain power and control. For such a person, sexual abuse may seem to be the answer. "It has been suggested that the sexual abuse of a child by a father is the ultimate act of anger toward his wife. It repudiates her validity and worth as a person, a wife and as a mother."[7] Abusing a child, a person easy to overpower, becomes easier than struggling to gain power with a spouse or peer. Abusing a child becomes easier than speaking out against a moral setting that restricts sexual gratification.[8]

Lack of identity: We all need a sense of identity, individuation, knowing who we are. Establishing a sexual relationship with a younger person reflects the appearance of being someone. At least the abuser can make it sexually with a child. Somehow in our society, a sexual identity has become more important than any other identity.[9]

Addictive personality: Patrick Carnes has described incest and sexual abuse as stemming from an addictive personality. The sexual addict is involved in a belief system resulting in an addictive cycle with four steps:

1. Preoccupation—the trance or mood wherein the addict's mind is completely engrossed with thoughts of sex. This mental state creates an obsessive search for sexual stimulation.

2. Ritualization—the addict's own special routines which lead up to the sexual behavior. The ritual intensifies the preoccupation, adding arousal and excitement.

3. Compulsive Sexual Behavior—the actual sexual act, which is the end goal of the preoccupation and ritualization. Sexual addicts are unable to control or stop this behavior.

4. Despair—the feeling of utter hopelessness addicts have about their behavior and the powerlessness.[10]

In addition there are three levels of addiction with differing behaviors, cultural standards, risks and public opinions.

Level one— Masturbation, heterosexual relationships, pornography, prostitution, and homosexuality. *Level two*—Exhibitionism, voyeurism, indecent phone calls, and indecent liberties. *Level three*— Child molestation, incest, and rape.[11]

This sexual addiction model has received much criticism on several grounds. First, it places sex as a form of addiction. Yet the removal of sex does not result in physiological withdrawal symptoms. Second, if an abuser is restrained from abuse, but allowed to function sexually, then what keeps him from going from stage one to the other stages of the addictive cycle? Clinical findings show no psychological or physiological data specific to sexual addiction.[12] Additionally, there are no moral or spiritual dimensions in this model.

Sexual compulsion: This theory suggests that an abuser lacks control over his sexual behavior. The proponents of this theory regard anxiety as the primary cause of the compulsion. The criteria for denoting a behavior as "compulsive" is highly subjective.[13] By labeling him *out of control,* the primary responsibility is removed from the abuser.

Deviance developmental sequence: In this model, the predisposition to abuse is caused by witnessing abuse and violence during childhood. Witnessing abuse results in a lack of trust, lowering of empathy and turning to self to have personal needs met. Antisocial and borderline traits, including perfectionism, inability to accept criticism, escape into fantasy, idealizing relationships, poor self-image with grandiose ideas, decreased trust and a need for structured situations, can develop.

Sexual preoccupation becomes a coping mechanism. As the fantasy becomes more and more uninhibited, the abuser may find a target on whom he can act out the fantasized sexual preoccupation. The grooming for the step of acting out, as well as the rationalized pattern of thinking take time to develop.

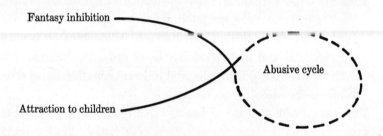

When the abuse, or fantasy, is acted out, the abuser withdraws. This physical or emotional withdrawal results in the need to start fantasizing again and compensate for the "down" feeling. Having learned the pattern of sexual escapism from childhood, the search for a victim starts again, and there is a lowering of fantasy inhibitions to the point of acting out again.

Types of Abusers

Just as there are different types of abuse, climates for abuse and possible reasons for abuse, so there are different types of abusers. These have been termed *fixated* and *regressed,* depending on primary sexual orientation and sociosexual development.

Fixated abusers are those whose sexual preference and involvement is exclusively with children or predominately with children while having only limited sexual contact with peers. Regressed abusers engage in sexual activity with younger sexual partners after sexual involvement with peers. Some regress if there is a breakdown with peers. Others regress only under extraordinary circumstances, and only for a period of time.

Gaining Sexual Access

Most abuse begins in very subtle ways. To gain the confidence of a child, a potential abuser can be manipulative, seductive and charming. Children have been taught for years not to take candy from strangers and to stay away from dirty old men. But strangers and dirty old men are not the most likely to sexually abuse children. Candy is not such an interesting enticement. The aggressors and their ploys are much more subtle than that, which makes it difficult even for adults to recognize the danger of the situation.

In a study of 250 offenders, thirty-one was the median age of the offender. Twenty per cent of the offenders were twenty years of age. Only ten per cent were over fifty. In seventy-five per cent of the 250 cases, the offender was known to the child's family. Various studies reveal that seventy to eighty per cent of abused children were abused by those they know, love and trust.[14] In many cases the offender used force, threat of bodily harm or misrepresentation of moral standards. Still other victims accepted with bribes of money or gifts. In some cases the child's natural loyalty or affection was subtly exploited.[15]

Here is one woman's account of her seduction as a child. As usual, her abuser's interest in her seemed harmless, even loving at first.

I grew up in a conservative Christian home. I was the youngest of four girls. We had a very loving family. Dad was a deacon, trustee, chairman of the board, boy's club leader and choir member. With all his responsibilities he was gone almost every evening.

Mom was tired after cleaning and general chores of a housewife. When we came home from school, we were told: "Go out and play." "Don't mess up the house!" "Don't bring home any friends; it will be too noisy." When I came in with a skinned knee, it was washed off, and I was sent back out with a cookie (instead of a hug and kiss).

I felt unloved. No one cared until my neighbor across the street said, "Come on over. You can walk our dog or help with some other type of chore." It was so nice to feel wanted. He actually wanted me around! He and his wife would take me out to dinner and buy me special gifts. It was great feeling special. He told me I was special and treated me like I was. This was never reinforced at home. He was a person I trusted.

When I was nine or ten, things began to change. He showed me lewd pictures. He wanted to see how I was developing. Before I knew it he was fondling me. He said, "Make me happy. Here, I'll show you how!" One thing led to another. I was *trapped!* I enjoyed this special time but somehow I knew it wasn't right. He told me, "This is our special secret. Don't ever tell anyone ever."

When I was fourteen, my father was transferred out of state. No one could understand why God would move our family from its roots of home. Praise the Lord he did. That's probably what saved me from the agony of this awful thing continuing. I have held on to the secret twenty-three years.[16]

One way abusers get children to cooperate is to make the abuse into a game: who can undress the fastest, who is the most ticklish, who can shoot the furthest, who will "feel the balls" or "lick the sucker." Offering physical gain, gifts and affection help keep the secret hidden in children who lack these securities from other sources.

To make sexual contact possible and to hide it, abusers work hard at finding reasons to be with children without other adults present. Abusers may feel more comfortable interacting with children rather than other adults. Often, they become possessive of their claims. This is especially seen in cases of incest when adolescent daughters desire to start dating. There are cases where abusive fathers continue the abuse of their daughters even after the daughters marry. The abuse only stops for some when they run away. Others find it difficult to marry or remain successfully married.[17]

For example, Jean married, thinking she had escaped the horror of her abusive stepfather. She soon found herself caught between a jealous, physically abusive, drug-using husband and a blackmailing stepfather. The truth surfaced only after Jean ended up in the emergency room after physical abuse, and her stepfather tried to have her committed for psychiatric treatment.

Pedophiles are generally gentle with children. Instead of being objects of abuse, the children are treated like people. Maintenance of an ongoing relationship is of interest to the pedophile. It is an investment of high emotions with a strong erotic component.[18]

Child pornographers sometimes do their work with the parents' full (paid) consent. Other times they work behind the parents' backs. These parents may sell their child's services as models, not knowing what pictures are being taken behind closed doors. One woman told of being photographed for a singing group while in an orphanage— innocent enough. The second set of pictures involved sordid sexual exploitation by adults.

Finding pornographic materials in someone's possession may be a good indicator of the owner's own sexual preferences. These materials are said to stimulate sexual involvement between the viewer and children. The correlation between sexual abuse and pornographic materials is debated, but results are not conclusive. Gebhard found many incarcerated sex offenders owning pornographic material.[19] Brown found forty-three per cent of victims involved in father-daughter incest were asked to pose for pornography. He also found that thirty-one per cent were asked to enact what they had seen in pornographic pictures, movies or books.[20] Although no causal connection has been found, we cannot be sure that a relationship between sexual violence and pornography does not exist.[21]

Although none of these examples include violence, some abusers do use violence in gaining access to a child. In a forced situation the offender uses behavior calculated to give him control over the victim. In some cases the aggression may become eroticized, with the offender experiencing excitement and pleasure by hurting the child.[22] The child may also be a target for the abuser's anger. This anger may not be directed against the victim, but the child is used as an object for its release. This group of abusers may include those who commit sadistic assaults involving torture, mutilation and murder.[23]

Types of Incest

We have dealt with the characteristics of the sexual abuser in general. I can understand defensiveness on the part of some who think that we have unfairly used examples of male perpetrators. But most reported abusers (data indicates over seventy five per cent) are male.[24] This figure may be distorted because in cases where a mother knows about the abuse and allows it to continue, she is labeled as a sexual abuser in some states. Brown, who did an extensive study with only females, found only one per cent abused by females. This may be due to reluctance of reporting victimization by females or the ability of female incestuous offenses to be more easily explained away.[25] An analysis of official national reports between 1976 and 1982 states that seventy-seven per cent of the perpetrators were parents (fifty-seven per cent being biological parents).[26]

Father-daughter incest is the most common incestuous situation.[27] While he is expected to be a protector, provider and loving parent, he goes over the line. One can see that without proper parenting and understanding of normal child development, a man could develop intimate interests in his own daughter. He would expect her to trust him, to cooperate, to not question.

The abuse usually starts with the oldest daughter—if there is more than one daughter in the family. Eventually, it can secretly involve all of them. In some cases fathers have not admitted guilt because they thought it their right and responsibility to initiate their own daughters sexually.

Father-son incest is said to be more common than mother-son.[28] Mutual masturbation among adolescents may not indicate an abnormal sexual preference but only the extension of natural curiosity. But a man forcing masturbation, oral sex or anal penetration on a young son is incest.

Cases of mother-son incest are reported, but rarely.[29] Whether this is because it rarely exists or just is not talked about is not clear. Mothers involving sons in this manner are those either having extensive nurturing drives or needing "a lover." Mother-daughter incest is considered rare.[30] Whether the increase in both the number of single mothers and the acceptance of homosexual lifestyles will affect these numbers remains to be seen.

In the past, sibling incest was not really considered as much of a problem. But as more adult survivors and abusers tell their stories, more stories of sibling incest surface.[31] For some sibling perpetrators, the motivation is wanting to care for another sibling in an intimate way. Perhaps the activity becomes a comfort after physical or verbal abuse. Maybe it stems from sexual curiosity. Others may use sexual abuse as a power play. It must be realized that sibling perpetrators need as much help as others.

Uncles, cousins and grandfathers are other sources of incest. How often are children expected to hug and kiss their relatives or sit on a grandfather's lap! Children find it imperative to obey parents and to do the expected, yet sometimes they can instinctively tell that something is not quite right.

For example, one day a friend was talking with me about abuse. Her twelve-year-old daughter overheard part of our conversation. Breaking in, she mentioned how uncomfortable she was with one uncle. The mother, previously hesitant to talk about abuse, graciously listened to her daughter. Permission was given not to hug the uncle. After the daughter left the room, my friend confessed that she had been abused as a child by that same uncle.

On the fringes of incest are live-in boyfriends, stepparents, stepbrothers and stepsisters. Already emotionally affected by divorce or other family trauma, their lives may be ripe for sexual abuse.

The characteristics of abusers are not limited to those described in this chapter. But I hope those given will help you be aware of possible abusers. Whoever is the perpetrator of sexual abuse, there is no excuse for this ongoing crime against children, a violation that will follow these children through life. Whether a perpetrator commits a single abuse and keeps it secret, commits numerous abuses in a gang, justifies the abuse as part of a cult's activities or publishes the abuse as literature or art, the abuser needs hope and help. But unless the perpetrator is recognized and stopped, proper help cannot be given.

—6—

Characteristics
of the
Abused

—

*B*e a clown. Hide behind the mask. Put the walls up high. Don't let anyone know. These are some of the ways that victims deal with abuse. Many of these emotions were captured on paper by an adult trying to live with the devastating effects of sexual abuse. The following is her poem:

Hiding
I hide myself behind walls so thick that even raging
 giants couldn't break through to me, if they tried.
And all the while I sit on the other side,
 between two worlds, both of which seem unreal.
Reality is only a thing from which to run away . . .

create a world of laughing smiles.
Inside, you're crying all the while,
    And so, within my soundproof walls, I hide myself away.
Why let people in to know you?
        Friendships only end in hurt. A broken heart is hard to mend
        with Band-Aids and Bactine.
Inside, the scar's still there . . .
        And so, I hide behind my wall, a clown with color-painted
        face. It covers up the tear-stained cheek,
But never can erase.
        In my corner, cocooned within the unreality of who I am and
        who they think I am, I sit.
But somewhere, deep within my soul,
    Buried with memory's debris,
I discover I've lost each minute part
    of what was once called "me."
My hiding game suited me so well,
    But now,
        Has turned into my private hell—
            Without Reality.

—Rebekah Riskin[1]

The pain and agony does not disappear with time. No matter what age the victim, sexual abuse cuts away at life itself.

Knowing the consequences are so great, it's vital to identify the victims—or potential victims—of abuse in order to provide safety and help. But where should we look for victims? Girls between nine and eleven are the most frequent victims.[2] More than eighty per cent of sexual abuse victims are girls, according to the American Association for Protecting Children.[3] Another study determined that for every boy abused, ten girls were victimized in a sampling of 250 cases in New York City; the median age was eleven years old.[4] A study in 1981 placed the mean age at 9.4 years.[5]

This doesn't mean teens, or even newborns, are safe. Sexual abuse can strike both males and females, at any age, in any place. But by looking at the common social, physical and emotional indicators of sexual abuse victims, we will be better able to recognize victims so we can provide the help they so desperately need.[6]

Again, as with the abuser, these are only indicators—and not the only indicators at that. A child with many of these characteristics is not necessarily an abuse victim. These traits can spring from other sources as well. But finding a child with many of these characteristics is cause for investigation.

Characteristics will differ somewhat from what follows, depending on the growth and developmental patterns appropriate for a given age and sex. The earlier the abuse, the greater the trauma will be to basic steps in growth and development. Just as a child cannot run if she has never been permitted to walk, a child can't trust others if she has had pain in trusting parents or self. The trauma of sexual abuse on newborns has even resulted in death.

As you read this chapter you may identify with some of the behaviors even though you have not been abused. These may, however, be buried feelings that need to be discussed with a professional. It is possible that you have been abused in some way but do not remember it.

Mental Indicators of Abuse

Direct and indirect confession: A child's own admission of abuse is the most open indication, but caregivers should not expect such a statement. A young or frightened child may be unable to state the fact. However, adults *can* listen for indirect admissions. Sometimes the child will talk of playing new games with a relative or other person, a game perhaps about suckers, snakes or secret things. Or an older child might mention something sexual that happened to a make-believe friend or to "someone else."

Age-inappropriate sexual knowledge or activity: Doll play or draw-

ings that express explicit sexual details can be a warning that a child
has been a victim of sexual abuse. Many responsible parents teach
their children the names of sexual body parts, but not often would a
preschooler know how to go about intercourse. A child curious about
sexual activities with humans or animals may be wanting to know if
what has happened to her is normal. A small child wanting to be
involved or involving others in sexual activity may not be acting
normally, especially if the child shows knowledge of the sex act or
foreplay. Seductive activity, promiscuity and/or excessive masturbation are warning signs. Where did the child learn such activity?

Sudden change in grades: Daydreaming or fantasizing about escap-
ing an abuser or wondering what it is really like for other children
can consume an abused child's time. If a child loses time in fantasizing, or if he or she cannot concentrate due to emotional upset, the
child's grades may drop drastically. On the other hand, grades may
quickly improve. Perfectionism expressed in this and other ways may
be the child's way of hiding the secret. It may also be done in an
attempt to avoid further punishment by sexual abuse.

Social Indicators of Abuse

Fear of specific persons or situations: Especially when a relative or
friend is the abuser, a child may have a hard time overcoming fear
because she was harmed by someone she thought she could trust. The
fear could be expressed in anger, sickness, nervousness, withdrawal
or lethargy. Talking about such fear is not the only indicator. A young
child may be very clingy or regress to a clingy stage inappropriate for
his or her age. A child who didn't mind being away from parents
before the abuse may be fearful of leaving home or going anywhere
alone after the abuse. Others may fear being alone. This could be
caused by fear of further abuse or by the pain of the memory.

Unusual modesty: An abused child, especially a teen, may not want
to change clothes in the girls' locker room at school or attend slumber
parties because undressing means exposure of physical signs of abuse.

Panic may result at the mention of a physical examination or trip to the doctor. Extreme reaction to even partial bodily exposure to family members expresses fear of the secret being exposed. Or an abused person may not want to uncover what he or she considers dirty and unclean.

Role in the family: Forty-five per cent of the women in Herman's studies had a major "maternal" role by eight or nine years of age.[7] In some cases the mother was sick or frequently absent from the home.

An abused daughter's relationship with her mother can be estranged, at times intensely so. This could be caused by a number of factors, including the child taking the mother's lover or the child's anger at her mother for not providing protection from the abuser.

On the other hand, there could be an unhealthy father-daughter bond. The abused may be seen as a "favored child" by other family members. This position may hold benefits, but the child likely feels a price has been paid in exchange. If only the truth were really known!

Antisocial behavior or running away: An abused child may become a loner so that no one can do him or her any further harm. The child may think that a price must be paid for every friendship. The child might have superficial friendships, but he or she may find becoming close to others difficult. The child may not develop friends to protect the secret of the abuse or because the child never had a chance to learn basic social skills before the abuse began. If the child expresses a lot of anger (due to the abuse) toward family and friends instead of the abuser, those relationships can become strained.

Hiding, running away and truancy are also social indicators of abuse. Why does a child not want to be with parents, friends or teachers? Emotional escape may not be adequate to keep away from the pain. The only true escape is to run. This is a request for help. A child doesn't run away or even hide under a bed, in the closet or at a friend's home without a reason. The ultimate example of running away is suicide.

Unusual dating behavior: Dating normally begins during adolescence, but abused teens may push it aside for the above reasons or because the abuser threatens the victim, stopping any interaction with suitors other than himself. Teens may also develop homosexual relationships to experience closeness without the pain caused by sexual abuse.

On the other hand, abused teens may begin dating prematurely or become promiscuous, perhaps more because such behavior is familiar than because it is enjoyed. They may also use this as an escape from their abusers, using intimacy as a source of comfort or a means of livelihood. Finally, the teens may see themselves as "used—free for the taking," not realizing they have the option to say no.

Exclusive relationships with elders: The constant private companionship of a specific older person could be a warning sign of abuse. Perhaps it is a young boy who is the constant companion of a boy three to five years older. If they always need to be alone and are possessive of each other, there may be cause for concern.

Physical Indicators of Abuse

When sexual abuse has taken place, physical signs may or may not be present or they may be hidden by the abused or abuser. Fear of finding such signs can lead to more brutal action such as murder or abortion.

Adolescents are especially vulnerable to the physical signs of sexual abuse—and their stress can be compounded if they don't understand the normalcy of menstruation. As in my own case, when my menstrual cycle began, I feared that it was caused by the abuse and kept the fact from my mother as long as I could, fearing it would expose my father's abuse.

Pain and irritations: At first the physical indicators may be slight, as the abuser prepares the victim for further abuse and penetration. Redness and irritation around the mouth, vulva or anus may appear. Physical pressure may cause hematomas or soft-tissue damage around the mouth, breasts, buttocks, genitals, thighs and abdomen. An abused youth may shy away from physical activities that could cause pain, such as riding a bicycle or a horse.

Genital irritations, bleeding or rectal trauma or suspiciously torn or bloodstained clothing should raise questions for parents and other caretakers. A child's having difficulty eliminating may be a sign of pain or embarrassment; she may think that anything from the private parts is dirty. Regression to bed wetting could also be caused by fear, irritation or trauma.

Infections: Constant infections of the throat, mouth or gums may indicate oral sex. Infections of the urinary tract, vagina or penis can be a constant bother because of abuse. Venereal disease has now become a widespread indicator of abuse. Pregnancy often forces a girl to admit to abuse, and when she is afraid to name the father it may be due to sexual abuse or incest.

Indirect signs: Frequent headaches, stomachaches, vomiting or loss of appetite can be brought on by revulsion from oral sex or the pain of penetration. Excessive weight change, as in anorexia or obesity, can indicate abuse, because a victim may be trying to become less attractive to the abuser.

Self-mutilating behavior: Self-inflicted burns, cuts and bruises or using harsh douches are a few ways that victims may cry out for help. They may be signs of trying self-punishment, cleansing or even of trying to see if they were still alive or capable of feeling pain. Two victims have described their behavior following abuse:

> I took several showers each day, never feeling clean. I started using Lysol, or anything else I could find, to douche. I felt that it must have been my fault that my father and men from his plant raped me. If I could only get clean, then maybe they would leave me alone.
>
> There were times I jumped from chairs or walls trying to break a leg or other bone. If I did succeed, then my mother would stay home with me, so my father would not use me. Instead, when I was sick, it was minimized or my father would take care of me only to reabuse.[8]

Emotional Indicators of Abuse

Self-destructive choices: Attempted suicide, frequent accidents, drug abuse and alcoholism are just a few of the self-damaging ways abused children may react to their pain, guilt and shame. Self-destructive behavior such as abortion or suicide can be a way of getting rid of the evidence.

Fear and mistrust: The social and physical indicators of abuse are interrelated with emotional indicators. These are not as easily defined in children. Fear and mistrust of others is prevalent. The fear can grow so intense that a child may completely withdraw, not only physically but emotionally. It is not uncommon to hear about out-of-the-body experiences or emotionally fading into the wall to escape pain.

Unprovoked crying or depression: Hysteria or spontaneous weeping can appear as well. There is a reason for crying—the pain just can't be put into words. Crying may occur at inappropriate times, triggered for seemingly no reason. Something that reminds the child of the abuse, such as reading a book, or watching a movie, may trigger tears. It may also occur during a happy event, such as a party, when the child's emotional guard is down and the emotion that needs to be expressed is suddenly released.

The emotions during the abuse may be so confusing or overwhelming that a child may not cry. A victim may dissociate from her feelings completely. Thus lack of tears when tears would normally be considered appropriate may indicate a deeper problem.

Unexplainable depression needs to be explored. Depression may be the only way to handle the pain of abuse. The anger is turned inward since the victim thinks it is inappropriate to be angry at others.

Regression to earlier phases: Developmental regression as seen in clinging behavior expresses fear. It is wise to know what is normal age-level behavior for a child and consider each child's behavior. A five-year-old who regresses to thumb sucking, a teen who reverts to nail biting and an aggressive teen who changes into a homebody are questionable behaviors.

Unusual nighttime behavior: Insomnia, nightmares and fear of the dark may be expressions of abuse. It is not unusual for abuse victims to have repeated dreams or nightmares of spiders, ghosts or snakes, of choking or smothering, or of a big black ball coming toward one's face.

Perhaps they are not dreams but rather the child's way of describing a sexual attack. The child may want to stay awake or keep the light on to keep danger away. Insistence on wearing underclothes to bed is a sign of protection for the child.

Excessive expressions of guilt: Always making excuses and inappropriate apologies may be another indicator. For some reason the victims assume the guilt for all they have suffered. They feel as if they caused the abuse. At times it appears that the victim tries to carry the responsibility of the world on her shoulders. The smallest mistake may result in panic from a victim. It is not unusual for an abuse victim to scrub herself all over in a bath four or five times a day, but the process doesn't make her feel clean.

It is difficult to say what effect sexual abuse will have on a child. The age of onset of abuse, the length of the trauma, the number of abuses, the amount of physical and emotional trauma coupled with the sexual abuse, and the relationship of the abuser to the abused all play a part in the results of the abuse. But no matter which way we look at it, sexual abuse will have an effect. Whether the abuse is a single incident or lasts for years, some characteristics and effects may always be present.

Personality Traits of Victims

A trusting child may be gullible to the offender's bribes and games. A submissive child will be easily threatened, going along with demands and directions from older, authority-type figures without questioning. A compliant child will go along with an abuser—perhaps to be accepted. An assertive child may approach a stranger, even go to them with open arms. An assertive child may escape from the abuse, but be in danger of physical retaliation from an angry abuser.

There is no one type of personality which lends itself to victimization. Focus on the personality of the victim may inadvertently place the blame on the victim, rather than the perpetrator. Personalities are still being developed during childhood. Thus, personality traits play a more significant role in the victim's response and in the formation of his or her adult personality than in the abuse itself.

We may be teaching children to be "safe" victims. Some people believe that girls should be passive, weak and opinionless; in other words, they should remain in a childlike state. They are to look to men for physical and economic protection. This means not developing independence, but rather remaining fearful and inhibited. They also learn that sex is to be used in exchange for support and protection. We teach boys to be fearless and strong. If they are abused, they must endure the pain without complaining so as not to appear afraid and weak.[0]

Where Abuse Can Lead

Whether the abuse remains a secret or is revealed in childhood or adult life, it has already landed its blow. This is not to say that every person who has been abused will show blatant signs of abuse. Yet some results of abuse cause most people to unknowingly further punish the abused person, rather than offering compassion or help.

The American public, especially within the evangelical community, has been quick to criticize behaviors considered unsociable or abnormal. They write off certain types of individuals as worthless blights on society. Unfortunately, some of these individuals may, in fact, be expressing the untold effects of sexual abuse.

It's important not just to note the effect and try to solve the problem (such as the runaway syndrome, drug abuse, prostitution, pornography, delinquency and crime) but to see beyond the offense to the possible root cause behind the behavior. Sexual abuse can produce unresolved anger, purposeful self-destructive behavior, a need to be self-supporting to get away from an abusive atmosphere and other catalysts for crime. Or the abused child might never have been given the opportunity for normal social growth and development and does not know how to cope with the reality of everyday living.

It would be shortsighted to assume a runaway prefers excitement on the street to living with loving parents. In 1979 alone, sixty thousand calls to the National Runaway Switchboard were received from girls and boys who had been sexually abused at home.[10] Other individuals and organizations working with teens are finding that many youths run away from home to find safety and a life away from abuse. No wonder some runaways cut off contact with their parents and even change their names.

As we've already noted, drug or alcohol consumption are often used to dull the pain of abuse. The unfortunate outcome is often that use becomes addiction. Further complications come as children try to pay for their addictions. Unfortunately, this cycle is all too common. Incestuous families are shame-bound, suffering from many types of addictions. According to two researchers, this results in addictive/compulsive behavior such as chemical dependency and eating disorders.[11] In an Odyssey Institute study, forty-four per cent of 118 female drug abusers were victims of incest.[12] In another study, twenty per cent of forty victims of father-daughter incest became drug or alcohol abusers, as compared to five per cent of twenty females in a group whose fathers made only seductive overtures.[13]

In a country where it's still possible to believe that child prostitution does not exist, six hundred thousand child prostitutes are sexually exploited annually.[14] Commercial sex, in the form of prostitution, pornography or both, involves 1.2 million children under the age of sixteen yearly.[15] In Los Angeles at least thirty thousand children a year under the age of eighteen are involved in the sex industry.[16] In San Francisco, a survey of two hundred current and former prostitutes revealed that seventy-eight per cent entered prostitution before adulthood. Ninety-six per cent of the young prostitutes were runaways. And sixty per cent of these two hundred reported being sexually assaulted before age sixteen.[17]

Delancy Street Foundation work with over one thousand prostitutes found a consistent pattern of sexual abuse in their backgrounds. Two-thirds were abused by father figures. The majority also had a religious upbringing, with seventy-six per cent attending church or church school regularly.[18] Twenty-nine per cent of seventy-nine young male prostitutes were sexually abused as children.[19]

Hundreds of minors involved in child pornography were interviewed in two recent studies by the National Center on Child Abuse and Neglect. Between half and three-fourths reported a history of sexual abuse within the family.[20] Incest victims, as revealed in Russell's extensive study in San Francisco, are over twice as likely to pose for pornography as non-incest victims.[21]

There are several factors to consider regarding prostitution and pornography. Many victims of abuse have the thought that once abused, always abused. It is a learned behavior. Sex is one thing the child knows she can do. It may be her only means of support, and she may feel destined to nothing other than being used as a sexual object in life.

But even if prostitution or pornography is a free choice, where did the child learn such behavior? And who hires, pushes or uses these children? Who shares their guilt?

In a decade-long study of over five hundred rape offenders, more than eighty per cent were found to have been sexually abused as children. In comparison, twenty per cent of men incarcerated for crimes other than sexual ones had been sexually abused as children.[22] Fifty per cent of female children in one reformatory in Maine had been sexually molested previous to their institutionalization.[23]

Russell also devotes an entire chapter to incestuous abuse as a contributing cause of revictimization. Out of a total of nine hundred eighty women sampled, sixty-eight per cent of the incest victims in her study reported rape or attempted rape by a nonrelative at some time in their lives as compared to thirty-eight per cent of the never incestuously abused.[24] Eighty-two reported some type of serious sexual assault. Close to three times as many (or twenty-seven per cent) reported a physically violent husband.[25] Fifty-three per cent reported unwanted sexual advances from unrelated authority figures such as a doctor, teacher, employer, minister, therapist or policeman.[26]

By giving statistics about the effects of sexual abuse on potential crime and delinquency, I am not trying to justify anyone's criminal actions. I *am* trying to suggest that preventing sexual abuse will help prevent a host of other ills later on. Studies giving data about sexual abuse and its long-term effects have just begun. It's possible we have only seen a few of the ramifications of abuse. In the remaining chapters, I hope to go beyond looking at this problem and suggest some concrete steps for aiding the abused.

—7—

The Dilemma
of
Disclosure

———

*S*uspicion or knowledge of abuse without taking action to stop
it is counterproductive. This may not only allow the abuse
to continue, but it sides with the abuser. Take Lynn's story, for instance. . . .

For as long as Lynn could remember, she had been exploited sexually. An adopted child, she at first thought her new parents had
rescued her from a very difficult orphanage situation. Instead, she
found herself having to sleep with her new father and be available for
his sexual gratification.

Sundays were spent at church where her mother was active. On
Friday nights both of Lynn's parents were involved in Satanic wor-
ship. Lynn was used not only for her father's gratification, but for her

mother's and others' in the cult. Frequent pregnancies ended in baby sacrifices.

When not sleeping with her father, Lynn was kept in a shed and prostituted to many men. One summer she was even sold to a family in another state, where she was locked in a trailer and prostituted.

Lynn tried at least two different times to seek help. During junior high school she told the school nurse who had befriended her about the sexual abuse. The nurse promised to stop it. The nurse then approached Lynn's father, who denied the accusation. Instead of help, Lynn received even more severe physical abuse. On another occasion, while working as a camp counselor, Lynn discovered that she was pregnant. She went to a home for unwed mothers instead of returning to college. Trying to find placement for Lynn and her infant, the home as a last resort called Lynn's parents. The parents came for Lynn, and the baby fell prey to their actions.

No wonder many like Lynn seek no help. Some never whisper a word about their abuse. Before we can consider the steps to help a victim of sexual abuse, we first need to understand the pressure a child feels to keep sexual abuse a secret.

Incest is said to be the "best kept secret." Most cultures have a taboo against incest. Some experts say the taboo is not in the experience itself but in talking about it.[1] With the increased attention that sexual abuse is getting from the media, our society must consider that sexual abuse is either on the rise or simply being reported more, perhaps because children are being taught by schoolteachers and the media to report "wrong touches" and abuse. Yet many children still choose not to tell.

Why a Child May Choose Nondisclosure

Herman says that the child both longs for and fears disclosure.[2] There are a number of possible reasons for children not disclosing the secret of sexual abuse or incest.

A child prefers the situation as it is: A child may not want to tell because she wants to protect the abuser, her family and life as she knows it; she dreads exposure of her supposed guilt; or she enjoys the rewards of the situation, however small they may be.

Disclosure disrupts the fragile equilibrium of a family that is tightly interlocked emotionally. Such a structure often resists change. Even if a child's present life is terrible, it may feel better than unknown changes that would result from admitting the abuse. Because revealing the abuse often means a girl must implicate her father, there's a chance that in his anger he will hurt the girl's mother or perhaps her siblings. She may fear the results of telling will be a shattered family, no one to turn to, and anger from Mother and society. Telling would reduce her father's image in the family, church, workplace and community. It would make the whole community privy to family secrets.[3]

Many never tell because of guilt. What started out as fondling did not seem serious. When it progressed to the girl sucking the man's penis, it involved her own actions—she was the guilty one, even though she may have been told "all girls do this with their daddies."

For example, after Charlotte Allen was raped in a park, her mother told her everything she supposedly needed to know about sex. Her mother told her dozens of things not to do, such as "never sit on a public toilet seat," "don't get into cars with strangers," "don't accept candy or money from people you don't know," "keep your dress down," "keep your knees together" and "don't go alone into a public toilet."

But her mother didn't tell her not to be used by her father! At first Charlotte's father gave her gifts and fed into her pride at being able to keep a secret better than anyone else. Gradually as she wanted to reveal the secret and she actively participated in the sexual experience, he changed his tactics.

During his sexual attacks, her father convinced her she was guilty and filthy. He placed a mirror between her legs and forced her to look at herself. He told her the names of the parts attached to the physical and emotional pain. It was as if she were repulsed by looking at an open wound. She despaired of the secret. She hated lies and feared being thrown into jail if others found out she was the one who was guilty.[4]

There seem to be some specific areas of fear and guilt for children who are taught to obey and trust God as a heavenly Father, to honor and obey their fathers and mothers, to tell the truth and to avoid the sin of promiscuity. Many children probably are not yet able to discern when disobeying parents (or any adult) would be the right thing to do, the will of God. Society looks down on "sneaking," and an adolescent finds it difficult to differentiate between honorable and dishonorable telling.[5] She violates a trust relationship if she discloses the secret in any way. Both telling and not telling the secret are sins.

Some children keep abuse a secret because the relationship between the victim and the abuser is the closest thing to a caring relationship the victim has. The child receives special favors. Sgroi found that the satisfaction of rewards and bribes, as well as the guilt and fear of blame for accepting them, kept many from telling their secrets.[6]

Some children do enjoy the sexual experience. A premature introduction to sexuality by a significant other may be enjoyable. In some cultures, it is expected. A first sexual encounter in our society is seen as an important rite of passage and sign of maturity.[7] It brings with it sexual pleasure, self-esteem, importance and a grown-up feeling.

A child is unable to tell: A child may be unable to tell because she has no channels for sexual communication, because she has suppressed the memory of abuse or because she doesn't know what is happening to her.

Often there is little or no valuable sexual communication within the home and thus no channel for disclosure, no vocabulary and little practice in sexual discussion. To avoid the embarrassment of discussing intimate sexual details, the parents never discuss sex; to avoid the same embarrassment, the child doesn't disclose an abuse.

Some victims try to pretend that the incest never happened. Sometimes they are able to deny and suppress the incest for many years. These defense mechanisms hide the aloneness, desperation, helplessness, feelings of being overwhelmed and the fear of the unknown. But even though the event has been "successfully" suppressed, a victim is not free of the negative psychological effects of incest. In simple terms, it is stashed on the inside but forgotten only consciously.

Adult survivors have the capability of working through painful childhood memories with adult strength and perspective. In later life, the victim may seek professional help for sexual identity crises, marital conflicts, depression or a host of other problems. The resulting therapy often brings the knowledge of abuse to light, and with it the reasons behind the problems. Fortunately, adult victims are often better able to understand the situation.

A child is stopped from telling: A child may be stopped from telling by the threat of violence, or by the belief (false or true) that she won't be believed.

Many children never tell because they are threatened with physical harm that would be worse than the pain of abuse. In a study by Sgroi, forty-six per cent of the abuse victims surveyed had been threatened with violence.[8]

Some children simply will not tell anyone, especially their mothers, because they feel they will not be understood, believed or sided with against the abuser. Telling anyone, much less the authorities, is not going to help.[9] For some this thinking may be the grim truth. According to Sgroi, even though the abuse was considered a secret, many family members knew and in some cases were also involved in the abuse.[10] Ninety-five victims of sexual abuse in Diana Russell's study offered unsolicited information on reporting their abuse. Thirty-seven per cent mentioned that someone knew about the abuse even without the victim telling.[11] The more distant the relation of the person who is told about the abuse initially, the more supportive the person seemed to be.[12]

Unfortunately, keeping abuse a secret can have long-term effects. The abused may become unsocial, isolated and unable to learn acceptable social skills. Identity and intimacy are not achieved properly.

Stressed family structures may remain. Fear of men and abuse in one's own family may occur. Antisocial behavior and suicide, among other self-destructive actions, are common. One can become entangled in a life of lies to protect her secret. I will always wonder about the aloneness of dying with such a debilitating secret.

Personality Differences

In the last chapter we established that the abused child's personality may be changed by the abuse. Dr. Ebrahim Amanat has conducted a study on the subject of rape response and personality traits.[13] The first of the three personality types is isolative, a loner. When abused, this person becomes more withdrawn, less trusting and aloof. Through fantasy, they continually relive the abuse. This type has the most difficult time reporting the abuse or asking for help. If these "silent" victims ever reveal their abuse, it is often not until adulthood, when it has already taken a psychological toll.

The second personality type is dependent, trusting and sure of being safe with the one they trust and imitate. After abuse, this type becomes more dependent and clinging, wishing to be taken care of. These victims also have increased phobias and nightmares and may develop substance abuse habits. These victims give vivid accounts of the abuse.

The third personality type is independent and autonomous and the most at risk of the three types. Because they are outgoing, they are often wrongly accused of being flirtatious and are blamed for the abuse. Their response is intensely emotional with the desire that others respond in the same way. They give clear, detailed accounts of the abuse, often intellectualizing and exaggerating. Irritability, agitation, compulsive behaviors, depression, guilt, shame and, eventually, repression are also demonstrated.[14]

Reactions of male victims are difficult to predict, complex and widely varying. Specific common reactions are confusion/anxiety over sexual identity, inappropriate attempts to reassert masculinity and reliving the victimization experience. This replay is also a display of anger and masculinity by offending someone else.[15]

Because there are such varied responses to abuse during childhood and adult life, we need to be empathetic and take time to listen and understand the abuse victim in an objective manner.

The Effects of Disclosure—Conflicting Views

Even with the rise of admissions, Finkelhor suggests that seventy-five to ninety per cent of sexual abuse victims never tell. Often, those who do reveal their secret do so as adults, through anonymous surveys. Finkelhor presents two conflicting views of why some tell and some do not. His study supports neither the theory of McCaghy nor of Armstrong.

McCaghy says that a minor event balloons into a major trauma only *after* the secret is told.[16] Other people reinterpret or re-label the experience which at first carried no guilt. The impact of the sexual abuse is determined by the subsequent events. Finkelhor suggests that the large number of those not reporting incest in his study may have made an accurate assessment of their situation and made the right choice not to tell. They feared that the reaction of others to disclosure might have been anger and hysteria.

The second view is held by Armstrong who contends that not being able to talk about the abuse causes a permanent scar.[17] It means never being able to be reassured or to find out what others think about it. There remains a feeling of differentness and ineradicable stigma. Thus the victim is more traumatized. It seems to be a no-win situation. Either the havoc created by disclosure dwarfs the experience, or the pain of silence and internally experienced stigma is worse than the experience itself.

The data collected by Finkelhor in his extensive study with college students indicated that only about one-third of respondents told anyone about their experiences. Those who did tell fared no worse or better than those who did not tell. The data did show factors other than disclosure contributing negatively to the experience. A few of these were the age, sex and relationship of the abuser, whether or not force was used and the duration of abuse.[18]

There are emotional ramifications, whether or not disclosure takes place. I believe that disclosure with support is the healthiest approach for several reasons. If sexual abuse remains a secret known only by the victim and perpetrator, the result is continuous emotional build-up. It is like constant unchanneled negative energy doing internal damage. If abuse is disclosed, even in the most ideal situation, there is an emotional drain added to the initial trauma. Supportive disclosure allows for the once internalized emotional effects to be released through various channels and over years. The pressure of keeping a secret is also diminished.

Much more research needs to be done to understand the effects of incest. With so many cases remaining a secret, we may never have an unbiased sampling for study. One very limited, biased study of adolescent female delinquents who were sexual abuse victims indicated that few victims who *do* self-report experience severe socioemotional/behavioral disturbances as a result of the abuse.[19] James also conducted a study with female residents of a juvenile institution. Results of his study showed "great suffering after the incest is revealed due largely to the strong reactions that persons have against this act which still remains a taboo in most societies."[20] Both of these were biased samplings and are expressions of the variety of responses a female may have to sexual abuse.

In the case of sibling incest, the perpetrator is often a male with his sisters or younger siblings. Some parents who are aware of sibling abuse suppress the knowledge. According to Sgroi, even when the abused child tells what is happening, the victim is asked to keep quiet. Parents express concern about what the neighbors will think. Because the parents do not want to know, the abuse continues with further threats due to the disclosure. The lack of parental responsibility in such cases is said to be more traumatic than the abuse itself.[21]

What You Can Expect When a Child Discloses

Disclosure most often occurs during adolescence in one of two ways: purposeful or accidental. Normal biological, cultural and psychological changes seem to precipitate disclosure. With menarche, there is the fear of being damaged or becoming pregnant. For those who do not have intercourse until puberty, the stress of puberty itself may force disclosure at any cost.

As an adolescent becomes intensely aware of budding sexual feelings, she may see how these differ from her feelings toward the abuser. An adolescent may also become aware of society's repulsion to incest or sexual abuse. In addition, adolescents normally struggle for a measure of independence. Such a struggle may highlight the dependency forced on her by the abuser.[22]

As the female adolescent strives for independence, the abuser may force seclusion and restrict social life. The victim of father/daughter incest may see the abuser as very jealous and fear that the abuse may happen to other siblings as she gains independence and is less available to her father.[23] The adolescent may begin to see him as a narcissistic, controlling individual. As she becomes more interested in peer group relationships than in the imprisoning father/daughter dyad, she may tell the secret to gain more freedom.[24]

Accidental disclosure may result from suspicion by a third party who observes behavior change, physical injury, sexually transmitted disease, pregnancy or precocious sexual activity. At other times the sexual attack is accidentally observed. Some victims may simply have a slip of the tongue.

When a child discloses abuse, the disclosure may be nondirect, partial or full. An adolescent may choose the anonymity of a hot line to test the system, test the reality of her thinking, get some answers and find temporary help. If satisfactory, the child may make a full disclosure. Some females tell their mothers indirectly. If their mothers ignore them, they won't usually do anything else.

Once the disclosure is made, the adult who is told may choose to deal privately with the matter to avoid social pressure or to avoid exposing the child to the criminal justice system.[25] Validation of whether or not sexual abuse has occurred must be conducted in an organized fashion, and collecting evidence for criminal prosecution is not easy. A professional counselor may be brought in to help deal with the situation, but even the counselor may not know how to, or may refuse to, deal directly with the issue. Thus, finding the right counselor is vital.

In other situations, the adult who is told may choose to follow legal channels and inform the government authorities of the abuse. The authorities then take charge of the investigation and perhaps other decisions affecting the welfare of the victim.

The victim may again have a feeling of not being in control of her fate. She may feel that adults and outside authorities do not believe or understand her, and become defensive. She might hear, "It's all over now, so just drop it. Forget it." With a big denial system around the victim, it is easy for her to use only selective memory.[26] Well-trained authorities can be a tremendous help in disclosure and its aftermath.

The child often experiences an initial relief in discharging the burden of a long-kept secret. An adolescent needs reinforcement of her story and help in revealing pertinent facts.[27] She needs support for her decision to disclose, and relief from guilt. If the disclosure was an accident, the child needs anxiety relief as well. Disclosure increases the likelihood of violence and desperate behavior. The family needs protection, especially the victim.

The abuser usually denies the abuse and tries to undermine the victim in any way possible. He is alarmed and threatened, struggling to maintain the power position. He may exploit his power position on the child and/or other family members. He may try to attack the credibility of the child or try to neutralize the effects of the abuse.[28] It is not unusual for the perpetrator to blame the victim by saying that seductive behavior led to the abuse.

Disclosure usually means separation by either removing the victim or the abuser from the home. With this the mother and other family members may blame the victim for not telling them sooner and for breaking up the home. The suppression state, as Sgroi calls this, may also include isolation by "ganged up" family members. The adolescent may run away, skip school or be involved in peer sexual activity. It's also common for those involved directly or indirectly to distance themselves, removing themselves from any setting that may remind them of the abuse. It is a means of stepping back emotionally to keep from feeling the painful memories. Blaming and distancing detract from the healing process.

Very few abuse cases ever go to trial. For those that do, disclosure means reliving the experience in the courtroom. It might mean further harassment at school and in the community. Recanting is common if the needs of the victim are not met or if the pressures are too much to endure. She may feel she is the betrayer of her family and be engulfed with both guilt and grief.

Helping a Child to Disclose

Disclosure is only the start of a whole new phase for a sexual abuse victim, in many cases a phase almost as difficult as living with ongoing abuse. Probably, the victim was traumatized by the abuse and her attempts to keep it secret. Now she will be faced with the trauma of disclosure and its aftermath. The victim's treatment after disclosure will probably affect her whole future.

So what can you do when you suspect or have knowledge about the sexual abuse of a child? Here are some steps which, if followed, will help the abused. Similar steps will be given in chapter eight for helping the abuser and the family touched by abuse. There are three crucial factors that should be a part of every step to come: sensitivity to the abused child and others involved, accuracy in gleaning and reporting details, and swiftness in reporting the abuse and any further abuses to the proper government authorities.

1. Believe any child who volunteers information about being abused.

A child does not usually lie about such an event. And the younger the child is, the more credible her story is. A child under the age of eleven could not gain sexual knowledge from fantasy. She must know from experience.[29] Even if the child were lying, it would be better to err on the side of caution and safety than to allow abuse to continue. Appreciate the intense feelings the person is experiencing and applaud the courage of the victim.

This step may sound simple, but sometimes believing a victim costs a great deal. Denial is far simpler. After all, if there is no admission of a problem, then there is no need to help! When Susan Brownmiller told her mother directly about the abuse she had suffered during a dental appointment, her mother accused her of concocting the story to avoid returning for another appointment.[30]

While some mothers believe their children, often they refuse to take action. After all, the mother has little to gain and everything to lose in believing her husband has abused their daughter.

2. When you are first told, learn as many details as you can about the abuse. More than likely, the child will share with you only some of the things she experienced. Be careful, sensitive and unhurried. This means listening to the child and others involved (if you can talk with them without jeopardizing the child's safety). Listen not only with your ears, but also with your heart. Make notes as soon as possible. Do not pump the child for details. Let the child use her own words. Don't suggest information and then ask the child for a yes or no answer. Be careful not to supply adult vocabulary. The child's own descriptions will be more credible as evidence, and hearing words like *promiscuous* and *prostitution* could cause the child to accept false blame.

It is not necessary for you to know everything in order to report expressed or suspected abuse. Don't take the investigation into your own hands rather than reporting it to the proper government authorities. You may do more damage than good by trying to be an amateur detective.

3. Consider whether the abuser might have had other possible or potential victims, perhaps in varying stages of abuse. If so, the same steps will need to be followed with them as well. You or government authorities may need to investigate; the other children may not be as willing to admit the abuse.

4. Without making the abuser suspicious, take steps to temporarily remove the child from any further danger until government agencies can intervene.

If the abuse has been perpetuated in the child's home, outside authorities may set up a new housing arrangement that separates the abuser and the abused. Be ready to support the child emotionally in the new situation. Being in another setting, unfamiliar to the child and away from known, trusted individuals, may give the child further trauma.

5. Report the abuse to your state's Department of Child and Family Services or designated hotlines. Be sure to have on hand as much of the following information as possible: child's name, address, phone number, age, school, parents' names, addresses, phone numbers, parents' employers, name of alleged abuser, address, names of other children in the situation who might be affected and need protection.

If you merely suspect abuse, try to determine if there is evidence of abuse that needs to be reported. Gently confront the child with your suspicions. If the child denies being abused, but your suspicions remain, it is appropriate to contact your state's Department of Child and Family Services and ask them to determine whether or not an investigation should be made. Children will often deny abuse for the same reasons they choose not to disclose it.

Hotline calls can be anonymous. Call for help or advice on what to do or *not* to do.

6. If you have not already done so, prepare the child for interviewing with the Department of Child and Family Services and/or police investigation. Remember that once the report is filed, investigation will be made as soon as possible, within twenty-four to forty-eight hours. Explain that the people who come will ask questions so that they can know how to protect and help her. Encourage the child to tell exactly what happened. Take time to be sure that the child understands that she is not the guilty one, that she is not "bad." The secret will only be shared with people who need to know in order to help and protect her. Be honest with the child—no more secrets!

7. When the authorities come to interview the child, do what you can to make the experience less traumatic for the child. You might be able to suggest a comfortable place for the child to talk with department workers and police investigators.

Once the investigation is in progress, find out if you can request a report of the investigation to determine what legal action is underway. Parents, legal guardians and, in some cases, the one who made the report of suspected child abuse are allowed copies. In most states you will need to make your request in writing and have it notarized.

Be realistic about the limitations of government agencies. With the increase of reported abuse, they have overwhelmingly heavy case loads. Be supportive of their work and their difficult task. If you think something has not been taken seriously, state your concerns.

8. Help the child understand that the sexual abuse was in no way her fault, regardless of the false guilt she might be feeling. Contradict the thought that the victim seduced the abuser. Try not to lay blame on other family members for not helping the child. Accusing these people may make the victim more defensive and cause her to decide not to disclose. Also, it will probably take time for these people to accept their part in the situation.

If possible, help the victim understand why she could not say no to the older person who abused her. (A child does not have the same mental, social, emotional and physical resources with which to fight an adult.) Stress that the child will receive help so that she can fight the effect of abuse and possible further victimization.

You may assume that latent sexual gratification is not often the reason the child allowed the abuse to continue. Most of the time, the victim feels only fear and pain in underdeveloped sexual organs. To block out the abuse, most victims try to deaden their feelings, not enjoy the experience.

9. Find the child a network of support people as soon as government authorities are contacted. Identify significant people in the child's life with whom you may form the support network. These may be family members, a school counselor, youth workers, friends or others. Try to include a professional or someone with previous experience in reporting abuse. Do not overlook the case worker from the government agency who will be assigned shortly after the investigation begins.

Bearing in mind the confidentiality of the situation, discuss what the child needs. Share your concerns with these people, and pray together for the child and for wisdom and sensitivity for yourselves.

10. Offer to help find a professional psychotherapist for the child and the family. Some states provide—and may require—counseling.

Please don't assume that because the abuse is over, the victim should automatically get on with life. It's not that easy. There is not only the trauma of the abuse but myths and stereotypes to contend with.

Work to help the child and those around her to avoid two false and damaging beliefs: first, that abuse is so damaging that the victim can never recover from the experience; and second, that abuse so impairs the victim that she can't function, rendering her memories, perceptions and thoughts profoundly distorted.

11. Be available—especially with a listening ear. Be alert for signs of progress or repeated abuse. It could continue even if the child denies it.

12. Make sure you have worked through your own sexual issues. Early sexual memories, confusion, anxiety and preference need to be dealt with before you will be able to help a victim. Only in this way will you be able to listen, support and provide helpful suggestions and information without coloring the experience with your own issues and bias.

13. Be patient. The steps in getting legal intervention in child sexual abuse are lengthy. It may not go the way you expect. The suspected abuse may not be founded. If it is, the case may be long and drawn out. This may mean being available as a support system at inconvenient times and for longer than you had expected. The days, months and years can be draining, but worth it in providing hope and help for the abused. It's only as the secret is disclosed and action taken that the vicious cycle of sexual abuse will stop.

—8—

The
Other
Victims

———

*M*arcos called a counseling center for help after attending a church seminar on sexual abuse. He said that his sister had been abused, and he wanted to get her into therapy. She had agreed to come one time if her brother could be present.

During that first meeting, it was obvious that she did not want help. She made excuses by explaining that it was her senior year of high school, and she would be going off to college.

During that session, however, Marcos admitted to molesting his sister and apologized to her, making the first steps in his own recovery. Marcos requested to return for further counseling.

In the next few months many changes took place. Marcos remembered sexual fondling by an aunt when he was about six years old. And he was able to tell his story of being raped at gunpoint on the job as a police officer. One of the results of the abuse for Marcos was his need to regain personal power. In time his struggle for power diminished, and he no longer brought a gun to the sessions. Later he was able to make a change to a job not requiring the use of a gun.

A struggle with self-identity continued for a while, but the intensity lessened when he was finally able to move out of his family's home and live on his own. Forgiveness of self was also a gradual thing for him. Eventually, Marcos became involved in a church ministry where he felt support and acceptance from new friends and was able to share Christ's love with others.

Because Marcos had found healing and a new type of power, he also knew that he had to wait for his sister to find help on her own terms, when she was ready.

Once the abuser has been identified, it is important that he, too, is given help—and more than just incarceration to prevent future abuse. It won't be as easy to reach out to him, but God has a better way for him, as well as his victim.

Reaching Out to the Abuser

That better way may begin with your own ability to have compassion for the abuser. This may be easier in light of Dr. Nicholas Groth's findings.[1] In almost a decade of working with convicted rapists, Groth has found that most of them were abused as children. Because of this we can empathize with them for they are victims too. Usually they were abused in their early teens. They thought there was neither hope nor help for them. Instead their need to express anger and power and their search for fulfillment finally ended in rape. If the rapist's situation did not change, in some instances the rapes increased to the point of brutality.

Clearly, a sexual abuser needs to stop. But he will need outside help to stop. Here are some steps you can follow in bringing justice, mercy and hope to an abuser:

1. Do not accuse the suspected abuser. The abuser is usually in denial. When a child accuses a person of sexual abuse, the child is usually telling the truth. The accused will be defensive, attempting to maintain control and power. Your position is not to convict. Appreciate the feelings of the accused. Be cautious but act purposefully. The emotional state and functioning of the accused are unpredictable. Even if the abuser self-discloses, do not accuse. Do let him know the serious nature of the allegations.

2. Listen to the accused. Be sensitive and unhurried. Do not make assumptions or place pressure on the accused. Make objective notes. Let the proper authorities do the interrogating. Don't try to take justice into your own hands.

3. Be alert to remarks or clues which may lead to suspicion of other victims of abuse. If so, follow the same procedure with the other suspected cases.

4. Provide safety for the abuser as well as the victim. It is so easy for a person accused of abuse to become a victim of public reaction. Place distance between abused and abuser to prevent further sexual or physical abuse. This may mean jail or alternative housing for the accused. The abuser may quickly be released on bail if jailed.

5. Report suspected abuse to the proper authorities. Encourage the suspected abuser to turn himself in to the proper authorities for help. Just because he says he will never do it again does not mean it will stop. Give the authorities all the information you have whether or not you think it is meaningful. Besides being your legal responsibility, this may bring the best possible help to both the sex offender and the hurting child.

6. Prepare the accused for investigation. Encourage him to be cooperative and truthful so that he can receive needed help. Let him know his legal rights.

7. Be available for the interview and legal proceedings if the accused requests this. Frequently, suspected abuse cases never go to court.

The accused still needs support even if the investigation is limited. Be aware that the investigation might also be time consuming, not moving as quickly as some would hope to insure proper justice.

8. Help the accused to focus on his responsibility in the abuse. Denial, blaming and minimizing are common defenses. Allow the accused to have a safe place to tell the whole truth. Be firm in the accused owning his behavior and not changing the focus to the victim or other people. The accused may need re-educating and sensitizing to see his part in the abuse since he may be unaware of distorting the situation.

One incest victim received this letter years after the fact:

We've never discussed the past but I want to ask your forgiveness if I have been part of the hurt and harm in your life. I was so ignorant as a teen-ager to the facts of life and many other things. I don't remember much of anything. . . . I do need your understanding and forgiveness if—I just don't remember. . . . Please remember me in your prayers—I need strength to continue my faith in the Lord. Talking to him is my only source of strength and hope.

Another victim confronted her father decades after he abused her. It was their first contact in many years. The letter did not accuse him. Rather it explained what had happened to the daughter. In response, the father wrote that he had many years ago forgiven his daughter for what *she had done to him!*

For both these abusers, denial has become a way of life. The first abuser had repressed the incidents so much that he had a hard time believing the events even happened. The second was able to deny that the abuse came from him at all.

9. Hope that the abuser will change, but know that this will not always happen. Plans may need to be made to keep the abused and the abuser apart indefinitely. For instance, the woman mentioned above who wrote her father happened to meet him again not long after they exchanged letters. The father again, as during childhood, made sexual remarks, placed his hands on the daughter's hips and tried prolonged, sexual kissing. He hadn't changed! It was twenty-five years after the abuse.

10. The accused will need support people. It is important not to just let him sit behind bars or be shunned. Family members or significant others may be helpful, but in many cases are not available. Persons who have themselves been abusers may give confrontive support. Confidentiality is essential to prevent overreaction from the public. Once the offender accepts responsibility for his behavior, he may experience a sense of guilt and remorse. This may lead to major depression and self-destructive behavior. Support, but do not rescue.

11. Be alert for opportunities to assist the abuser in seeking help through psychotherapy. This could involve individual or group counseling. Professional help can provide opportunity to identify underlying reasons leading to abusive behavior. It can also provide alternative coping skills for stressful life demands. Confession and forgiveness do not negate the need for professional help.

12. Be available. Consider how the church might become involved in the therapeutic process for someone outside the church. For church members who are abusers, consider the meaning of restorative, redemptive discipline and healing relationships. The book by John White and Ken Blue, *Healing the Wounded,*[2] is an excellent resource on exercising church discipline.

13. Be patient. Working with offenders may be lengthy and unrewarding. The offender may resist help. A person in mandated treatment will not be as receptive or motivated as a self-referred offender. The rate of relapse in some offender programs is low, but it would be erroneous to think an offender can be permanently cured.

Disclosure, no matter how it takes place, is the only way the healing process can start. Disclosure allows the emotional defenses to drop. It is only then that the victim, abuser and others can perceive the emotional dimension of abuse. For some at the point of disclosure it is as if the lid of a garbage pail has been lifted. To others it is like bursting from a cocoon. It is here that we start to identify with the pain and emotional dynamics of abuse.

The Family of the Abused or Abuser

As we have seen, there are those cases where a parent or family condones abuse once it is discovered. Terri came from such a family. When Terri was thirteen years old, her father started abusing her. When Terri told her mother, her mother forced Terri to continue having sexual relations with him because she didn't want to satisfy him herself. In such a case, both parents need to be seen as abusers and both need the kind of help outlined above. But there are many parents and families who need a very different kind of help once the facts of abuse are brought to light.

Watching the results of sexual abuse can be very painful. For a caring parent, it is as if a fragrant rose is withering away petal by petal without explanation. When the abuse is discovered, these parents endure a variety of emotions—anger at the abuser, pain for their child, grief over a lost childhood, guilt for not protecting the child, and the shock and embarrassment that such a situation would strike their family. Most parents are never prepared for such a traumatic experience.

In the following account, a woman named Laura shares insights into what it is like to be the loving parent of an abused child. How would you help this woman?

A friend called to see if he could visit us for a weekend. He was in town for business and as often before, he called us. Family life with us would be a welcome change for him from a hotel.

He had been my husband's roommate in Bible college twenty years ago. He is a very fine, respected person in his community, an excellent church leader, an elder, a club worker and a boys' Sunday-school teacher.

Somehow I felt very uncomfortable on this visit. Because he used unusual eye contact with me, I felt extremely uneasy. It was as though he could see right through my skin. As the weekend progressed, he proceeded to make obvious sexual advances toward me. My gut feeling alarmed me.

I regret so much as I think back that we left our children home with him for an hour and a half on Saturday afternoon. He was so willing to baby-sit, almost demanding that we leave them home with him. He said we could have a little more time to be gone since he would be staying with them.

When we returned, I was aware that something had taken place. He himself gave clues that something was wrong. I watched as he put his arm around our beautiful eight-year-old daughter and said, "We have a secret."

"Why, oh, why didn't I go on my gut feeling?" I asked myself. Now I knew my suspicions were confirmed. I hadn't told my husband how I had felt earlier because I thought he wouldn't support or believe me.

Later that Saturday afternoon this trusted church leader went into the bathroom to watch our daughter take a bath! I was busy fixing dinner and didn't even know this had taken place until bedtime. My husband said to me, "What is bugging you? You sure seem uptight."

When we retired to bed that night, I spent the night in fear. We had left our house guest staying up watching TV. I didn't feel I could say anything to my husband just then, but where could I go if I didn't get the right response from him? Certainly not out with the person I had become afraid of. Instead of confronting anyone with my fears, I lay awake, mostly to be sure my children were safe. At one point my husband asked if I were still awake. I asked him to close the children's bedroom doors. I knew I would hear a click if they were opened. That night was, I'm sure, the longest of my life.

The next morning was spent as if nothing had happened. We went to church. During the "breaking of the bread" our guest, being an elder, got up to share some Scriptures. I taught my Sunday-school class during the second service.

That afternoon when my daughter and I were alone, I questioned her. She seemed scared and afraid. Something about her was different. The knot in my stomach was getting larger and larger.

After we took our visitor back to the place he was staying, I finally shared my feelings with my husband. He agreed that there was an uncomfortableness about this visit. Again our daughter denied anything unusual.

Months began to pass. We watched our beautiful, happy, spontaneous daughter begin to change. She became very angry, untrusting and explosive. Her excellent grades in school began to go down. Her behavior at school was also brought to our attention. Still she was very quiet about the reason!

Three months had passed. While our daughter was taking a bath she asked me if I would explain menstrual periods to her. It was a great time of talking and sharing. It gave me the opportunity to go over some of the facts that we as Christians tend to stay away from! Yes, I told her again that her body was her own and that no one was to touch her in an uncomfortable way.

That did it! She exploded in a flood of tears. Feelings of fear, shame and guilt began to come out of this once carefree child. Yes, she is only a child! Yet she had been treated like an adult with such violation.

I asked my husband to listen to the details of the violation this visitor had committed against her. My heart just broke. The grieving I felt, and *still* feel, is heart-rending. She told us that he had assured her that it was okay to do these things, saying, "I do it to my own daughter."

As I listened, hate, anger and guilt came to me immediately. How could this be happening to our family? to me? I too had been violated at the age of nine. My husband and I had wanted to protect our children from this awful, sinful experience. We couldn't. Why? We had told our children not to let anyone touch them and not to reveal their private parts. We told them never to be afraid to tell us if someone made them do these things. Why had this happened?

Yes, we went and reported it to the police. Yes, the Department of Child and Family Services was called in. We learned that because this "trusted" friend lives out of state, and since there was no chance for recurrence in our state, that he would not be extradited or put on trial! His state has been notified to investigate his activity with his six-year-old daughter.

Yes, even after a year the nightmare still remains: the fear of not being safe in our own home, the guilt I feel as a loving parent, the failure I feel. I know now that if you think there's something wrong, you're right.

What a great and courageous thing our daughter did in telling us! Her secret is out, and she is able to talk about some of her feelings with us. She has also begun therapy to heal the deep hurts that had been trapped by silence. With love, support, acceptance and prayers, we are beginning to feel there may be an end coming to our nightmare.

I still feel a great anger and hatred toward our visitor. I have questions about our court system. But I do have the assurance that God will punish him. . . . Please pray for us as we deal with our feelings. Pray that we will have an understanding of the sin that has affected our lives. Also that this may be used to God's honor and glory. Pray especially for me, as I deal with the great anger I feel not only toward the abuser but also toward our loving God.

Steps for Helping

Grief. Pain. Guilt. The loving parent or parents of a victim need immediate aid—to help their child and to deal with their own anguish. Here are some steps that will allow you to help the hurting family.

1. Treat the parents with the same care you would give any other grieving person. Expect the parents to feel shock, denial, anger, depression, a need to act and, perhaps, ultimately, acceptance of the

situation. But don't be too impatient for the acceptance to come.

2. Be available to help the parents make decisions that will bring healing to the child and justice and help to the abuser. In a case of incest, decisions need to be made that could jeopardize the family unit. It is important not to take all the responsibilities from the parents of the child. They already feel as if they have lost control and do not know who they can really trust. Help them seek professional advice, offer insights and alternatives, and then allow the family to make their own decisions.

3. Be ready to accept those fighting to survive the pain of incest in the family. It's easier to "be there" for families in which abuse came from outside the family unit. When the abuser is a woman's own husband, it's harder to address the issue.

4. Provide mediation. Immediate cessation of violence is essential. This may include crisis intervention or separating the abusive elements. Assessment can provide a clear unbiased perspective on the situation with the whole family's welfare in mind. Mediation may also mean immediate or short-term counseling and resource location.

5. Reduce or eliminate sources of stress that lead to violent reactions. This may take place immediately if the factors are known, or over time through counseling. If changes are abrupt, they may lead to more stress instead of giving the much-needed improvement.

6. Encourage counseling for the whole family. Counseling is needed on an individual basis as well as for one-on-one sessions for parents, mother-daughter, father-daughter, and so on. The abused person may even consider attending a support therapy group while the family attends group for added support and understanding.

7. Be aware of some of the dynamics of counseling and be aware that changes are taking place, but they take time. The following are some areas covered in counseling which may be reflected in a change of behavior, or unpredictable behavior until worked through:

☐ Self or inner awareness

☐ Identifying and labeling feelings

☐ Identifying basic behaviors and problem behaviors
☐ Appropriate expression of anger and grief
☐ Clarification of roles
☐ Skills to alter current behavior patterns
☐ Personal communication skills

8. Educate the family members. They all need new information and skill development. Assertiveness training may give a sense of self-esteem and protection. Parenting techniques may help bring some equilibrium to the family structure and gain of appropriate power. Anger management will alleviate stockpiling of anger which may explode into violence, abuse or self-destructive behavior if not defused. Communication skills are essential.

9. Be fair. Refrain from taking sides or using coercion. This may only lead to denial or hostility. The parties involved do not need to be judged by individuals, causing them to again feel overpowered or threatened.

10. Provide safety. This may mean temporary shelter for a victim or other family members. Avoid rescuing them, but provide a place for appropriate ventilation of feelings. Give a listening ear without a thousand-and-one questions.

11. Expect the family to change. Allow this to take place without over-expectation. This may mean prompting them when there is a lack of motivation. Remember that the problem will not just go away or not ever happen again as some would like to think. A gentle balance is needed to prevent dependency, rescuing and coercion.[3]

The Healing Process

Three charter members of a self-help program in California wrote the following creed after finding rewarding results. I think it aptly expresses what is needed in family healing:

To extend the hand of friendship, understanding, and compassion, *not* to judge or condemn.

To better our understanding of ourselves and our children

through the aid of the other members and professional guidance.

To reconstruct and channel our anger and frustrations in other directions, not on or at our children.

To realize that we are human and do have angers and frustrations; they are normal.

To recognize that we do need help, we are all in the same boat, we have all been there many times.

To remember that there is no miracle answer or rapid change; it has taken years for us to get this way.

To have patience with ourselves, again and again and again, taking each day as it comes.

To start each day with a feeling of promise, for we take only one day at a time.

To remember that we *are* human, we will backslide at times.

To remember that there is always someone willing to listen and help.

To become the *loving, constructive* and *giving parents* or *persons* that we wish to be.[4]

There are many victims of sexual abuse who need help. Some are seen, some unseen. It is important in the process of helping that you know both your own power and your limitations. You may be a powerful agent in healing by being well informed and by directing victims to those who you know can help.

The following account expresses the pain of a woman who is both the mother of the abused and the wife of the abuser. Linda was herself a victim of childhood sexual abuse. So she has pain on pain. Here she explains the help she desires most from the body of Christ.

It would not take much for you to become acquainted with me. I am a middle-aged, divorced Christian woman trying to provide for myself and three children. . . . I struggle "normally" with my singleness, finances and adjustment to change. There is, however, the not-so-obvious side of me, the secret hurt that is not understood and certainly not "normal."

It has been said that sexual abuse is one of the "best kept secrets," and it is easy for me to see why. The secretiveness is perpetuated for me, in part, because of the fear of people's responses
when I tell them. But I feel that if I never share my secrets with
you, we both lose a lot: I never give you the opportunity to minister
and you will never touch my hurts.

I will never forget the day my sister called and told me that my
husband had been sexually abusing her son, my (then) nine-year-
old nephew. I will also always remember more recently having to
take my young son into the police station for questioning on the
sexual advances of his father. My husband was a minister, and I
knew that dealing with the problem would ruin his career and ruin
all my dreams. I had been aware of his problem for a while, but the
fact that it was so close to home finally forced me to acknowledge
the reality of the situation and take action. I have told very few
people the details of why I'm divorced, even though this means I'm
taking responsibility and blame by not revealing the facts.

It would help to have you respond to me in four important ways:

☐ Please respond to me with the *integrity of your feelings*. Be
real. If you are shocked, angered, repulsed or saddened, express that
feeling. If you show some feeling (even negative) it shows you care.

☐ Please respond to me with *knowledge*. Learn as much as you
can about sexual abuse and be able to ask me sensitive and intel-
ligent questions.

☐ Please respond to me with *eye-to-eye contact*. Do not look
down or away from me. I will see in your eyes your level of care.

☐ Please respond to me with *consistent friendship and warmth*.
Be careful to be as friendly and warm to me after you know as you
were to me before I shared.

—9—

Healing
for the
Abused

——

I *don't think I can ever trust a man again!"*
"I'll kill my father if he tries it again!"
"I hate my mother for not protecting me!"
"Suicide is the only answer. There is no way anyone would want me after what he did to me."

"No one, not even God, could love me with all the guilt I have. I feel so dirty!"

"I still love my father and want a baby by him. I know it isn't right, but I still feel that way."

"I don't understand or trust my sexual feelings anymore. I'm so confused! Is being a homosexual the only choice for me?"

Children may have the feelings behind these statements but not have the words or concepts they need to verbalize them. More often these are typical responses of adult incest survivors. Survivors? Yes, because they are alive and learning to live new lives, often using the help of therapy to resolve their issues.

You may ask if professional treatment is really necessary, especially for those who have the Holy Spirit of truth as Counselor (Jn 14:16) and who can turn to God for wisdom (Jas 1:5). Because this has been for years the most common opinion held by Christians, the church has left the abused and abusers to depend on God alone. But this is a Catch-22 situation since the abuse has made it difficult for them to relate to God in the first place. As a result, victims have most often gone without help, and abuse has continued into the next generation.

Such a person often rejects God the Father because he is seen as the Overpowering One rather than All-Powerful One. John G. Finch says that he does "not know of a single Christian in therapy, whose relationship with his father being bad, was able to accept God's love."[1] A therapist with religious training and sensitivity to the spiritual dimension of a person can be of help to this type of client.

Psychological treatment of sexual abuse victims has come a long way since I was an abused child. How well I remember the psychological testing I received after I told of my abuse. The tests seemed prolonged and illogical. No therapy followed because the tests determined that I didn't have any psychological damage as a result of the abuse. But that's not how I felt inside.

As the years passed, hidden issues came to plague me. As a child, I was relieved that I didn't receive therapy, but in retrospect I wish I had gotten treatment. I wish I had been heard and guided by someone who understood what it felt like to be abused. In later years I was able to receive such help from trained therapists and group-therapy members. The help, hope and strength I received through therapy has allowed me to help others and write this book.

Amy is another Christian who is receiving help in later life. She has described her experience:

I know that sexual abuse is a subject that makes many people very uncomfortable. Nevertheless, I believe that because abuse exists, it is something which we need to deal with. Why is it necessary that we deal with it? Why can't we turn our heads from it, hoping that "it will go away"? The answer to both of those questions is that there are so many people who have been abused and have been carrying that hurt inside themselves all alone for many years. The emotional hurt and pain that comes as a result of sexual abuse is very deep. That hurt and pain does not "go away on its own."

My abuser was my pastor. He gave me a lot of attention, gained my trust and then took advantage of me as a teen. I don't think it is necessary to go into more detail, except to say that it was a very confusing time for me.

I kept it a secret until I was thirty years old. I had begun having various physical problems, yet there was no medical reason for them. I was also suffering from depression. My doctor, who is a Christian, wisely suggested that I talk with someone whom I could trust. I began seeing a Christian therapist. It was in the beginning of therapy that I knew I had to let the secret out and start dealing with it in order to get well.

I vividly recall the day I told him. I had never told anyone before, and it was extremely difficult for me to talk about it. Once it was out, he began to skillfully and wisely help me work through the pain—emotional, physical and spiritual pain. I am so thankful that he has had the knowledge and the ability to help me in all of these areas, but especially that he has had the sensitivity needed in helping me through many spiritual struggles.

My perspective of God had been terribly distorted. I have experienced tremendous doubts and fears about God—doubts such as: "Does he really exist? If he does, does he really care about me?" It is extremely difficult for me to see and feel his love. I would like to feel free to ask God to show me that he loves me, but I'm afraid to ask—I'm afraid of what he might do to me in order for me to experience and feel his love. I struggle with wanting him to use me, and yet I also struggle to believe that he can because I have all of those doubts and fears.

Just recently I have made a decision to make a deliberate, positive response to certain situations. For instance, when a situation occurs in which someone else would find it clearly obvious that God is saying he loves me, I will tell myself that *I want to believe* that God is showing me his love even though I feel uncertain about it. I hope that in time this will go beyond being an intellectual decision to becoming a genuine belief.

I wish I could say that I have completely worked through all of this. I haven't yet, but I am in the process of doing so. For me, the process has been slow and discouraging at times, but I'm thankful for family and friends who have lovingly supported me even when I felt like giving up. Because I have talked with those who have had similar experiences and have "come out on the other side," so to speak, I have hope that I, too, can experience freedom from the bondage that abuse has brought me.

In recent months I have become involved in group therapy with other Christian women who have had similar experiences. This has met a tremendous need in my life. I have experienced loving acceptance and support from them.

There are well-meaning people who say, "Just turn it over to the Lord." As I've said, I believe they mean well and I want to believe that they desire to be helpful. Yet, I don't think that they fully realize the depth of the problem. Their comment suggests that the problem will vanish with one simple decision. That type of advice usually heaps a tremendous amount of guilt on a person who is already hurting.

I am not saying that the Lord cannot do anything to heal the effects of my abuse. He knows and understands everything involved in this type of issue. Therefore, I believe he uses those people who are knowledgeable and qualified in this area to help those who have been abused—just as he uses medical doctors to help those who have physical problems.

Perhaps you are asking yourself what you can do to help someone who may open up enough to tell you he or she was sexually abused. I have a few suggestions. Listen lovingly and patiently without being judgmental. Let the person know that you care. Encourage the person to seek professional help from a qualified Christian therapist. I hope and pray my words will give you new insight into this sensitive issue.

Amy stresses the help that therapy can give an abused person. The abuser and the family can receive the same needed help. Presently there are new programs being tried across the nation for all three groups. These programs may use individual, group or family therapy, or a combination of all three. Each participant usually sets his or her own goals. For instance, the abuser may want to come to the place where he can admit guilt and take the blame away from the victim. Families may look for the underlying causes which precipitated the abuse. Through therapy, individuals and families can learn to communicate and correct situations which may have led to the abuse.

The appropriate therapy style and length of treatment will vary from person to person. Individual therapy is often best for the intensity of the initial crisis, and it can act as a bridge to group therapy.[2] Group therapy can instill trust between participants and therapists.

Adult groups for abuse survivors provide a place for them. Group members often show a special kind of understanding because they have been through the same ordeal, and they can challenge each other to work on issues. A support group run by and for survivors offers members a chance to help and be helped. Such groups can be inexpensive or free and sometimes can involve more people than other groups can. Individual and group therapy can be led by men or women, survivors or nonvictims. Each can have special effectiveness, depending upon the needs of the person seeking help. As with physical treatment, each person's emotional treatment must be custom-designed to that person's treatment issues.

Specific Treatment Issues for the Abuse Victim

Porter, Blick and Sgroi[3] suggested ten impact and treatment issues for victims of sexual abuse:

1. "Damaged goods" syndrome
2. Guilt
3. Fear
4. Depression
5. Low self-esteem and poor social skills
6. Repressed anger and hostility
7. Impaired ability to trust
8. Blurred role boundaries and role confusion
9. Pseudomaturity coupled with failure to accomplish developmental tasks
10. Lack of self-mastery and control

Though these ten categories may not encompass every abuse victim's needs, they represent the experience of most child abuse victims and abusers. I will use these ten basic treatment issues to present findings that are based on interviews with abuse survivors and therapists and on my own experience.

I will be noting some Scripture verses that have been helpful to me. But because a victim of abuse often perceives Scripture from an altered perspective, please do not automatically present Scripture verses to a person seeking hope after abuse. Try instead to encourage with Scripture and to help the individual work through irrational beliefs. Concentrate on modeling God's loving concern for the person. The fact of God's love is often extremely difficult for a victim to grasp in other ways. Make sure your love includes acceptance of the person and confidentiality concerning whatever the person shares with you.

"Damaged goods" syndrome: Almost every victim of childhood sexual abuse feels damaged by the experience, whether physically, emotionally, socially or spiritually. I call this the "garbage pail feeling."

Victims can perceive such an image because of physical damage, infection or injury. They often describe themselves as a piece of garbage, something rotten. One survivor told of actually climbing into a garbage can after her abuse. Another wanted to destroy herself by climbing into a garbage bag to suffocate. She felt that if she threw herself away, no one would miss her.

Many victims experience physical damage through abuse. They need to express their perceptions and knowledge of their own bodies and what took place. Such conversations may bring painful memories, especially if there was bodily injury, physical pain or pregnancy. Try to offer support as well as guidance to correct any misconceptions of cause and effect regarding the abuse. For instance, a girl who started menstruation without understanding why it occurs may consider it permanent damage caused by the abuse, a monthly reminder of trauma. There can be similar misconceptions about pregnancy, abortion, physical examinations, future sexual relationships or female surgeries.

For example, as Caron underwent testing and surgery many memories of abuse and her helplessness came back to her. Having a nasalgastric tube put through her nose to her stomach resulted in gagging like the gagging that occurred when she was a child after having forced oral sex with her abuser. A rectal exam required the positioning which her father used to abuse her and the familiar feelings of a lack of privacy. X-rays reminded her of pornographic exposure. Having a mask placed over her face made her feel as if she were suffocating from her abuse. This resulted in a whimpering crisis like that of a small child as she recalled the painful memories of a life shattered by abuse. Only professionals equipped to understand the emotional, as well as the physical, complications of the abuse could help her through this ordeal.

Most victims also experience damage in their relationship to society. Unfortunately, society often perpetuates the "damaged goods" syndrome. If a victim's abuse is known, she may be shunned by her male and female peers and the community. For this reason, many victims

question whether or not to tell a date or a spouse about sexual abuse
for fear of rejection and further condemnation. In my case, for many
years I had a hard time wearing white, except in connection with my
nursing duties. Every time I thought of marriage, I wondered if I
could wear a white gown—or would I not be allowed to because of the
abuse?

Though some members of society may shun an abused girl, others
may consider her a "walking invitation" for sexual gratification. To
them, the abuse was a rite of passage that helped the girl to "come
of age." This response may be even more damaging than the first
because it perpetuates the abuse at the hands of more and more abusers.

Perhaps the national awareness of the sexual abuse problem will
change the general response of society. Obviously, victims need significant people in their lives to behave very differently toward them,
neither condemning the victim, nor condoning the abuse.

The adult survivor needs to be supported in the positive social
interactions she has had in her life. You may be able to help by
sharing statistics that show her she is not one of a kind—there are
others who have been injured through abuse. Help the victim meet
other survivors, especially those who have been able to work through
their abuse and become successful in a way that is meaningful to
them. Help the survivor decide how open to be with the fact of her
abuse, knowing the different reactions society may give her.

Try to be careful how you respond to the survivor through facial
expressions and tone of voice. Try in every way to communicate acceptance and respect. Physical touch that is not sexually stimulating
can help *when the client is ready*. This can be a big step in removing
the feeling of "uncleanness."

Most victims experience spiritual damage as well, often fearing they
will never be holy, pure, righteous or clean before God. A victim may
feel that God's standards can never be achieved no matter how hard
she tries; therefore, she may feel rejected by God. How could such a

person ever feel forgiven and a part of God's family? This is especially difficult if the abuse continues.

This person may not have enough faith of her own. At least for a while, she may need to depend on your faith that God has a positive plan for her life (Jer 29:7-14), that God never abandons his children (Ps 138:8), and that he redeems and renews by his compassion and love (Ps 103:1-5).

Guilt: Even though the abused is the victim, she more than likely will feel she is the guilty one. If she has lived with this feeling for years, however untrue it may be, it will not easily be dispelled. She may feel guilty for the sexual behavior itself.

Since adult/child sexual behavior is not a societal norm, it is often conveyed in verbal or nonverbal ways that the child must have caused the abuse. A young child does not just happen to know or behave in a sexually provocative manner. It is learned behavior. A young child does not cause abuse to occur. Even if a child has learned sexually provocative behavior, it would still be the perpetrator's responsibility to prevent the sexual activity. Try to reassure her that she is the victim and is not responsible for the act.

She will probably feel guilty for disclosing the act and the effects it had on her family. Let her know about her rights to her own body, rights protected by laws in every state. Explain that any ramifications of disclosure (divorce, father's loss of job, public scorn, whatever) are the abuser's responsibility, not hers. Some therapists have joint sessions with those involved in which the perpetrator is asked to take the responsibility. If confrontation is not possible, the therapist may conduct a confrontation through a role play to allow the client to release her guilt.

Once the victim understands what behavior she is *not* responsible for, she may also need to learn what part of her behavior she *is* responsible for. Help her identify responsible behavior, if necessary, or direct the victim to a support group that can help her work through the rethinking process and gain self-understanding.

The victim may ultimately express guilt in self-destructive behavior, perhaps by damaging body parts which remind her of the pain. You may need to make a contract with the individual to stop such behavior and then check with the person periodically to make sure the self-abuse does not take place.

For a Christian, the guilt of abuse can be overwhelming. A victim may feel that that nameless "unpardonable sin" *does* have a name: experiencing sexual abuse. The victim may feel that no amount of asking forgiveness is enough. And it won't be enough because false guilt (a favorite tool of Satan) cannot be remedied by confession.

As the victim distrusts God or others, new guilt feelings come. And the abuse runs counter to many of the high moral standards the Christian holds: the wrongness of sexual behavior outside of marriage, selfishness for not wanting the abuse which is desired by the older person, resistance to obeying an abusive parent or adult, lying to cover up for the perpetrator, selfishness in enjoying the special attention after the secret was told, and anger toward the abuser and those who refuse to help, including God. Many times, anger is denied and is either turned inward to become depression or outward to become unacceptable aggressive behavior. The victim needs to know the shelter of God. The victim's abuser needs to know the forgiveness of God. Christ is our high priest and has already paid for our redemption (Heb 7:25-26; Rom 5:8-9; Ps 34:22; 1 Jn 1:9; 1 Cor 6:9-11).

Fear: Fear can be expressed in many ways, including recurrent sexual thoughts, nightmares and desires which may bring further guilt. Fear causes children and adults to do unusual things. An abused child may hide or run away. An abused adult may remain hidden behind perfectionism or isolation. Some have described the fear as having no place to hide no matter how they try to escape. These victims need to know a place of safety. An abuser may hide by being outwardly perfect, loving and kind. This person's only hope of peace is in confessing the abuse.

The victim's greatest fear is often of disclosure and the conse-

quences of such disclosure. The victim may fear reprisal by the perpetrator. Victims report visualizing the abuser's face at the strangest
times and in the strangest of places. They may fear the reactions
of family, church and community. Often they fear that permanent
damage was done to them, whether emotional, mental, spiritual or
physical, in the form of homosexual feelings, mental or emotional
instability, eternal separation from God, physical damage or future
disability. Many times the victim worries that the damage is incorrec-
table. It is easy for the victim to believe that some innate sexual
problem caused the abuse, the resulting rejection or later intimacy
problems.

First of all, the victim needs to know that the damage of abuse is
not irreparable. Then each fear must be identified and worked
through. It is appropriate to help pinpoint what are realistic and
unrealistic fears. In some cases, more accurate information must be
substituted for mistaken beliefs. Establishing new trust relationships
will reinforce and strengthen the survivor's sense of safety. Again,
both the victim and abuser need to know their position in the family
of God. Remind them that God has brought them to the place where
help is available, and reinforce concepts of God's mercy, protection
and love (1 Jn 4:7-8; Rom 5:1-2; Ps 34:4; 2 Tim 1:7; Ps 111:10; 1 Pet
5:7).

Depression: Common before and after disclosure, depression is extreme in many cases of abuse and can result in self-destructive behavior. If the abused person suffering from depression were to draw
herself, she may picture a flat, empty body. The victim may experience
sadness, withdrawal, fatigue and complain of physical ailments or
attempt suicide.

To overcome depression, an abuse victim needs to perceive that she
is believed and supported as she ventilates feelings and that she needs
opportunities for this to occur. She needs to hear positive statements
about herself and life to help her through her self-defeating, self-
destructive or suicidal behavior. Professional assessment is needed,

especially if medication is necessary.

Christians may become depressed when they are unable to follow the advice "to just forgive and forget" or to be a "joyous Christian." When you work with abuse victims, stress that Christ asks us to forget the past and press onward. Part of forgetting means working through issues, not burying them alive. Christ himself wept as well as experienced joy. God created us with many feelings and the capacity for tears (Ps 34:18; Ps 43:5).

Self-esteem and social skills: One victim of abuse labeled herself "nobody," instead of using her name. Abuse undermines a person's self-esteem. A victim may feel unworthy and undeserving of anything. To protect himself from discovery or to keep the victim all to himself, an abuser often prevents the victim from socializing with peers. The victim therefore does not learn normal social skills. Negative feelings surface as disparaging comments or untrue beliefs about one's self. Some call themselves undesirable and set out to prove differently, with often disastrous intimate sexual relationships. Many go into prostitution.

The person needs help to identify and dispel the negative feelings she experiences about herself. Help the victim find her positive attributes. If the woman is attractive, help her see this by having her compare her positive physical features with photographs she considers attractive. Suggest "homework assignments" that will allow the person to experience success.

High self-esteem comes with grasping one's personal worth in Jesus Christ. The process can be helped by group support. Vibrant, growing Christians willing to be transparent and vulnerable are excellent role models. With such models, a victim can learn that she is created in God's image, loved unconditionally by God, eternally significant, infinitely valuable, indwelt and energized by the Holy Spirit, gifted for ministry, treasured as God's child and a necessary part of the body of Christ. But all this takes a loving, accepting body of believers who will give the abused person a chance. The same can be done for the abuser and affected families (Eph 1:17; Ps 138:8; Ps 149:4).

Anger and hostility: Each person expresses anger in different ways, not just through yelling or physical violence. Repression, transference, denial and conversion are common ways for the sexual abuse victim to hide anger and hostility felt toward the abuser and those who allowed the abuse to occur. Many times a victim has mixed feelings—love and anger, a desire to protect and punish the abuser. Anger can have positive effects. It may be the motivation for finally disclosing and ending the cycle of abuse. But anger poorly handled can be a time bomb waiting for detonation.

In repression, the victim may partially or totally block out the memory of the abuse, or remember—but blunt—the emotional effect of the abuse. It is not unusual for the repressed anger which has unconsciously been pushed inside to come out in other ways. When the anger is focused on other people such as counselors, teachers, people with similarities to the abuser or people who failed to prevent the abuse, transference is taking place.

At times a child has been so emotionally traumatized by the abuse that conversion—somatic or physical symptoms without a physical cause—may occur. Examples of these are paralysis, inability to talk or swallow, deafness, lack of sensation, lack of coordination or various kinds of unexplainable pain.

A victim's misplaced anger often lands on God. Where was he when he was needed? One researcher has found that most sexual abuse victims have turned from God because of this question.[4] Explain that God is certainly angry at the abuse, angrier than the victim is. Through his love, Christ experienced the abuse along with the victim. Christ himself paid the price of the sin on the cross. God will hold the abuser accountable.

The victim should be allowed to express those feelings in a safe, nonjudgmental atmosphere. Help her find nondestructive ways to vent her anger. Group therapy is a fine way to learn how other survivors handled their anger and to learn to relate to others positively in a controlled situation.

For the abuser, anger and hostility may be the underlying cause of abuse. The abuser may need help identifying and resolving the root of the anger, and then finding an appropriate resolution of that anger.

It is possible to get beyond anger to forgiveness. Recently, I was interviewed about my experience of abuse and how I had been able to forgive my father. A Christian in the audience insisted I should still be very angry at my father, implying that something was wrong with me for no longer being angry about something the Bible is against.

I could tell the interviewer was nervous about such a reaction to my story and shocked when I wanted to respond. I explained I did not like the abuse—I hated it and the effects it had had in my life through the years. I assured the man that I do believe in biblical principles, among them the message of God's forgiveness when there is repentance. God loves my father as much as he loves me, and he desires that my father have a right relationship with him.

Another biblical principle I believe is a Christian's responsibility to forgive others, for our mutual benefit. When I forgave my father, I removed an obstacle that had kept me from going on with my life. It meant that my father's actions no longer restrict me; I am not responsible for him. If I were to live my life in anger, I would be missing out on God's plans for my life. God did not plan the abuse, but God has used that horrible situation to allow me to learn more about life and God than I would have otherwise.

Forgiveness is one of the biggest steps in treatment. After the abused and others have had their anger affirmed, they may be able to begin the process of forgiveness. This next step may be a long time in coming. But it is as the injured parties forgive the abuser that God is given freedom to work (2 Cor 9:8, 11-12; Ps 90:14-15; Jn 20:23; Col 3:13; Mk 11:25; Ex 34:6; Ps 30:5; Eph 4:26; 2 Cor 2:10).

Trust: The victim may find trust a larger hurdle than almost any other because abuse can cause a victim to lose her ability to trust even herself, let alone others. Pressure from the situation may cause the victim to act in ways that seem to be against her own best interests. Family may give double messages or not support the person when the going gets tough.

Unfortunately, it is easy to shatter a person's trust, but hard to rebuild it. It takes time to rebuild trust. Often, the rebuilding can best be done through the vital support of concerned people and a therapist. Unfortunately, when victims have been abused by trusted individuals, it is hard for them to believe that anyone could be responsible and sensitive. Being patient and explaining procedures and therapy may resolve this. Allowing the person to have some say in the treatment program may help.

Abuse victims also have a hard time trusting God. It is difficult to trust his sovereignty, holiness, forgiveness and love. It is difficult to believe Scripture. Verses that some people find comforting can sound like accusations, making the victim feel even guiltier. Abusers with religious convictions sometimes use Scripture to justify their actions. If the abuser is a church member or claims to be a Christian, victims often see the person as indicative of all Christians and find it difficult to trust the church family.

Just saying that a person should or can trust God does not make it magically happen. By implying this, you may make the victim's guilt worse because she is doubting God. Victims and their families need to be given time to learn about God without being judged. Assure them it is okay to have doubts. Give them time to trust you, even if change seems to take forever. And listen. Be steadfast in your walk with Christ and don't give the appearance of being perfect. Be real and be open about the ups and downs in your faith. Give God a chance to work (Eph 3:16; Ps 62:8; 1 Pet 2:6; Ps 28:7; 29:15; Jer 17:7; Rom 10:11; Prov 3:5-6).

Blurred role boundaries and role confusion: "Who am I?" This is a common question for a victim of abuse. The victim may feel as if she is wearing a large sign that says "abused," "used" or "available." This belief comes from being forced into premature adult sexual experiences. The person becomes confused about what acceptable behavior really is. It will take retraining for the person to understand what is socially appropriate and age-appropriate behavior.

In some families the abused has had special privileges. Family therapy may be the only way of determining what are acceptable duties and privileges for each member of a family. A child who has become a little mother needs the chance to be a child again. If the victim is an adult survivor, a therapist may recommend play therapy to help the person experience the benefits of play for the first time.

The victim will need healthy relationships to replace the role of sexual partner to an older person. She can be helped to define the roles of her perpetrator and others in her social milieu. This, along with group therapy, will help the victim relate to peers in acceptable ways. (The abuser could benefit in the same way; an inability to relate to peers may have made sexual abuse attractive in the first place.) If married, the survivor may need help in understanding the role of the spouse and the fact that all people are not abusers.

Those of us in the Christian community need to offer the abused person other role models that can be the basis of a right relationship with God. If the person is ready to hear Scripture, offer verses that reveal God as a provider, protector, avenger and healer. God loves the victim and abuser unconditionally. Find nonsexual ways of expressing love to these people. Be God's channel of love (Ps 68:5-6; 116:6; 147:3; 1 Cor 10:13; Jn 17:15; Heb 10:30; Jer 30:17; 33:6).

Confusion and pseudomaturity: Not all victims have problems with their roles or the roles of significant others around them, but a sexual abuse victim is deprived of a childhood. She needs to understand this and be assisted in exploring areas of development that have been missed. The survivor may need help in understanding children and their developmental stages and needs. The victim may also have to clear up confusion about her sexual identity. It is healthy for a survivor to interact with a therapist of the opposite sex in a safe setting where the client will not feel overpowered.

Persons with independent or detached personalities have specific needs in this area. Both may feel that they can do it all on their own using intellectualism, or that the abuse does not really matter. The stoic becomes confused, feeling emotional pain and a need for comfort, but remains detached. The independent person may reject the help of others.

A sign of pseudomaturity is perfectionism and a preoccupation with rigid rules for living. For me, earning brownie points from God became a way of life. I needed to be perfect in God's sight, serving him as a missionary. I longed for joy and freedom in my Christian life, and I had that joy, but not often. It only came when I sensed that I was as perfect before God as I could be, yet I always seemed to fail.

Christians who are perfectionistic miss the freedom to enjoy God and a relationship with him. Some have an unsatisfying relationship with God but keep it secret. They may give themselves unreservedly to ministry or service but cannot gain any real satisfaction from their work for Christ. They don't understand that God alone restores the soul and refreshes. All our striving for perfection cannot achieve that sense of rightness and peace.

You can help perfectionistic Christians by making your life transparent to them and letting them see how you accept your own limitations, because you know that God sees his finished work through Christ in you. Abused and abuser may be able to overcome their desire for instant maturity if they see gradual Christian growth honestly expressed in you. Help them establish reachable, reasonable and realistic goals so that "perfect" isn't their only standard (Phil 3:12; Ps 19:7; Ps 23:3).

Self-mastery and control: One abuse survivor drew a rag doll dangling from marionette strings—a way to express her lack of personal control. Such a feeling is common for abuse victims. When a person has been long abused, she has usually been kept from making or carrying out her own decisions. This situation blights her will and thwarts self-mastery and personal control. Other victims turned to extreme self-control in areas they can control to cover up the secret or to ward off further abuse. Children or dependent people may have unusual needs in this area; young children must be treated according to their level of development.

Friends can give them opportunities to make safe decisions, a secure setting in which to risk, succeed and fail. Perfectionistic abuse survivors need to learn that perfection is no longer necessary for survival. The abuse is over; it is all right to make a mistake. In individual or group therapy, a survivor can experience acceptance and safety to try and risk. When she realizes nothing detrimental will happen to her with her therapist and group, she will be able to start relaxing outside of the therapeutic environment as well.

Victims and abusers who struggle with self-mastery may have trouble understanding the scriptural truths about the lordship of Christ. The idea of being controlled by the Holy Spirit could be extremely threatening. To such persons, common phrases like "Let go and let God" sound more like "you have no rights." To help them deal with these issues, carefully discuss their questions regarding the Bible and God, listen nonjudgmentally and try to help them gain a more balanced perspective of living a life based on biblical principles (2 Pet 1:2-8; Rom 5:2-11; Phil 1:6).

One researcher has summarized the losses of childhood and how they effect adult life. The results in adulthood are loss of control, safety, playfulness, trust, calm, self-confidence, self-esteem, sexual maturity, intimacy, comfort and security.[5]

The Grieving Process
The process of healing involves not only the above treatment issues, but also grieving over a stolen childhood. It is the process of realizing both the losses of childhood and adulthood as a result of the abuse. Denial, anger, bargaining, depression and acceptance are generally

considered to be the stages of grieving. Vacillation between these stages may continue for years.

Denial precedes the healing stage and may include forgetting the abuse, repressing the memory, numbing and putting up a front. During the healing, it may mean denying the amount of abuse, the effects of abuse, the definition of abuse and minimizing the abuse compared to what others experience. There may be the denial of the need for help.

Anger may take many forms. Before disclosure, the feeling of anger may be denied or misplaced onto others. It may be squelched and internalized. And the victim may become depressed or use inappropriate behaviors, such as substance abuse, for release. During healing, the anger may emerge uncontrolled. Alternative release-methods are helpful to lower the pressure. Monitoring of self-anger will be needed, as well as patient supportive help.

Before disclosure, there may be bargaining with the abuser through blackmail, threats or requests not to hurt others in the family. It can also mean bargaining with self, thinking, "It can't really be that bad if it is over." Bargaining during healing may mean agreeing to a set time of treatment only, giving up if something doesn't work right away or getting help only if the others who are affected get help.

Persons who begin the healing process will most likely experience depression, feeling worse before they get better. They may think that there is no way out. Emotions are like a black cloud around the person. It is important not to give up hope at this point.

Acceptance involves the victims recognizing that the abuse has affected their lives and that they need help. It means they accept the fact that they will never be the same because of the abuse, but that they can change and grow into a worthwhile person.

* * * * * * * * *

Although these treatment issues are not exhaustive, I hope they will provide a strong foundation for identifying and dealing with an abused person's problems. There will be nothing easy about providing that help. The person may reject you as she denies her pain and needs. But Christ would have you persevere because unconditional love may be just the thing needed to bring the survivor back to health and wholeness.

–10–

Healing for Abusers and Families

—

*A*lmost half of sexual abusers are under twenty years old.[1] The juvenile sexual offenders may suffer from feelings of inferiority, inadequacy, lack of self-confidence and maturity, have difficulty establishing satisfying relationships, or have poor anger management.[2]

The process of healing for the offender will include the same issues as for the abused, if the abuser has also suffered sexual trauma. We can get an idea of added issues when we consider the ten treatment issues for victims as they apply to the abuser:

Treatment Issues for Abusers
"Damaged goods" syndrome: The abuser may not feel that he or she

is physically capable of functioning sexually. He may be impotent or have other sexual dysfunctions. He may not have emotional and physical responsiveness to partners of appropriate age. He may feel he needs to function according to societal expectations, so he over-responds. He may need physical proof that he can function as a man.

The abuser needs clarification of appropriate sexual functioning, support if he is not able to function as he desires and a realistic assessment of his needs and means of gratification. He needs educating on sexual facts. He needs help with poor judgment, poor impulse control and clarification of misconceptions.

Guilt: Responsibility for the abusive act must be taken. When support without judgment is given to the abuser, he may then be willing to admit that he needs help, instead of denying and blaming. When the abuser does not know that what he did was sexual abuse or that it was wrong, clear messages need to be given. A combination of social justice and psychological help will continue this message of consequences for the injustice. The abuser needs to take responsibility for what he did not only to the abused, but other family members. Many never admit to guilt or remorse.

Fear: Fear of further accusations, real or false, may follow. A sexual offender may realistically have a fear of sexual or physical retaliation if incarcerated. Loss of family, friends, job and respect are also found. Even if guilty, the abuser needs to be given safety, justice and support by significant others and society. Only in a safe environment will he be able to move beyond fear to responsibility and healing.

Depression: It is not unusual for depression to occur when abuse is revealed. The abuser may resort to heavy drinking, use of drugs, or even suicidal or self-destructive behavior. Anticipation of such behaviors is needed as well as the availability of crisis intervention. Support is essential through this period, with guidance for working on responsibility and healing for the primary abuse issue.

Self-esteem and social skills: Re-education, resocialization, peer support groups, marital counseling, assertiveness training, sex therapy, enhancing communication skills and stress management are all ways of working with the abuser. He may lack social skills with his own age or social group. The abuser needs to have someone who believes in him and his ability to change. He needs to know God's forgiveness, and the fact that God can enable him to function despite past failures and sins.

Anger and hostility: Retaliation is often the response to accusations of sexual abuse. For this reason the abuser must be kept in a place where he cannot to be harmful to others. It needs to be a safe place where he can ventilate his anger. He will need training in anger management since rape or abuse is often a crime of power or anger. He will also need much support, without rescuing, in handling the anger appropriately directed at him for the abuse.

Trust: It would be erroneous to think that sexual offenders can be cured. Therefore, he must learn how to trust himself, when not to trust himself and when to seek help in taking responsibility for maintaining appropriate behavior. Trust from family members or the abused may never return. Any trust will take time to build. Part of this process is creating safe situations to start building communication. He needs help to get in touch with unmet needs that lead to the abuse and to learn alternative ways of having these needs met. Stress management will help him successfully cope with life demands. Help him identify and become sensitive to his patterns and characteristics that may be warning signs to further abuse.

Blurred role boundaries and role confusion: Re-educate on appropriate roles. This may mean strong role models. The buddy system is one way to help develop a sense of appropriate role behavior. Allow the abuser to talk about what he sees as his role in society and family in a nonjudgmental atmosphere. Help the abuser clarify what are realistic boundaries and expectations for him—not you. Allow him to grow and make mistakes, but provide structure to ensure not returning to inappropriate sexual behavior.

Confusion and pseudomaturity: The abuser may more likely be suf-

fering from lack of maturity, socially and emotionally. Find out where
he is in both areas, and help him develop skills to achieve his unmet
needs. He may be confused or unable to meet what he perceives as
social expectations on him leading to inappropriate sexual behavior.
Allow him to talk about these and help him set realistic expectations
for himself. Let him know set limits that he must not exceed.

Self-mastery and control: The abuser needs to know the responsibility he has to control his behavior. Behavioral training is helpful
here. Help him to see areas in his life that he has mastered, and give
him permission to excel in those areas. Enhance positive areas to
diminish the need for achievement shown through sexual abuse. Help
him learn parenting skills. Assertiveness training will also be of help
in this area. Provide places when he can be in control. Allow him to
know that he is not less of a man if someone else is directing him.
Allow him to make mistakes in areas without rejection or punishment
for not being perfect. Help him to understand the peace of God's
direction and control.

Treatment for Sexual Addiction

In the sexual addiction model a Twelve Step Program is used. The
belief is that a mental illness caused the abuser to be addicted to sexual
gratification. The first step for the abusers is a believing that they are
powerless over their addiction, and their lives have become unmanageable.[3] Helping abusers who are acting out sexually in an addictive
pattern will be time-consuming.

First of all, you must be frank about the consequences for inappropriate behavior. Then, allow him to openly discuss his fantasies, helping him to see the difference between fantasy and living out a fantasy.
Help him build new coping skills. Develop alternative attractions or
means of gratification. Find out what triggers the cycle. Build his self-
esteem, and do not allow him to withdraw. Emphasize *his responsibility.*

The following steps are adapted from the Twelve Steps of Alcoholics Anonymous particularly for sexual addicts.

1. We admitted we were powerless over our sexual addiction— that our lives had become unmanageable.

2. Came to believe that a Power greater than ourselves could restore us to sanity.

3. Made a decision to turn our will and our lives over to the care of God as we understood Him.

4. Made a searching and fearless moral inventory of ourselves.

5. Admitted to God, to ourselves, and to another human being the exact nature of our wrongs.

6. Were entirely ready to have God remove all these defects of character.

7. Humbly asked Him to remove our shortcomings.

8. Made a list of all persons we had harmed, and became willing to make amends to them all.

9. Made direct amends to such people wherever possible, except when to do so would injure them or others.

10. Continued to take personal inventory and when we were wrong promptly admitted it.

11. Sought through prayer and meditation to improve our conscious contact with God as we understood Him, praying only for knowledge of His will for us and the power to carry that out.

12. Having had a spiritual awakening as the result of these steps, we tried to carry this message to others and to practice these principles in all our affairs.[4]

Treatment Issues for the Family

These same areas are specific family treatment issues to work through when a family has been struck by abuse, whether by incest or someone outside the family system who was the abuser. These include:

"Damaged Goods" Syndrome: Social stigma within the community or church may be real or imagined. Those outside the family may have

a false impression that if abuse occurred with one child, then it *must* have happened to others. Actually, abuse *may* or may not have occurred with the other children. Siblings may think that they will be called names at school. There may be more social isolation on the part of the family or by the community. Family members may continue to label the victim as "bad" and not to be trusted.

These things may occur in various ways, such as not being invited to social functions, friends no longer being able to associate with each other, cessation of babysitting jobs, obscene phone calls or pranks. The family needs to sit down and talk about their feelings and reactions to the abuse. They need a safe place to talk about what is happening to them, not just to the victim. The parents need a separate place to talk as parents, as well as with the family, so that they may maintain a strong parental role in the family. Community education helps alleviate some of the stigma. Christian love is essential.

Guilt: One of the main family-assumed guilts is not protecting the victim or not knowing that something was wrong. The false guilt needs to be dispelled by talking and correcting misconceptions. This would also build family trust. The family can help the victim release her guilt as proper guilt is placed on and left with the abuser. If there are areas of guilt within the family, individuals must resolve these. It is important that family not side with the abuser or blame the victim. The family structure can become stronger and further abuse prevented by resolving guilt. Remember, forgiveness and leaving the abuser to resolve his guilt does not mean allowing him quickly back into the system if he was previously a part of it. Justice must take place. Change in abusers is possible, but not quick. Cure must not be assumed, even if the abuser says he will never do it again.

Fear: Fear is very real in the families of abuse victims. Unless the identity of the abuser is known and there is physical separation of the abuser from the family, fear remains that abuse will reoccur. There are also fears of the family breaking up, of stigma and that the cycle will continue to other family members—now or in future generations.

Fear of retaliation or physical harm if the truth is told by family members who knew about the abuse often keeps them in silent shame. Safety with recourse must be provided to talk truthfully. (This may take time.) Also safety must be maintained even if the family (in case of incest) is separated. If incest has occurred, then something is already unbalanced within the family system.

Depression: Depression may occur in family members. This may especially affect the parents of the victim. Encouragement and support will help them through this. Release of unexpressed anger will help prevent depression.

Low self-esteem and poor social skills: Many times incest occurs within socially isolated families. A buddy system or adoptive family will help provide friendship and a role model for social skills. Involvement in group functions will do the same. Refrain from a one-to-one buddy system without supervision, because incest victims are easy prey for re-abuse.

Repressed anger and hostility: Anger, hidden or known, occurs in family members when abuse has taken place. Often only professionals can help individuals identify their hidden anger. Education on anger management may be needed to help family members safely ventilate their anger. It is essential to help family members focus their anger in the right direction, not on the victim. Siblings and parents need to work through anger for the time, energy and attention the victim has received without the victim assuming false guilt. Safety needs to be provided so the abuser will not respond in anger or hostility to the victim or family.

Inability to trust: Careful planning and time are essential to rebuild trust within the family system. This involves trusting parents to protect, listen, not judge and to believe. It also means parents must learn to trust their own ability to guide and protect their children. Parenting group with effective parenting skills is basic. Regaining trust does not mean automatic trust of the abuser. This may take time, or may never even occur. Parents will need to help their children build trust in themselves so they can learn to function safely and learn age-appropriate individuation skills.

Blurred role boundaries and role confusion: This will most likely happen when incest has occurred. Family therapy will help the family to see how they are functioning and work toward appropriate balance. This process may be very painful with individual resistance. In some dysfunctional families placement of children in alternative living situations may be necessary to provide safety.

Pseudomaturity: Role modeling and family counseling will help parents with their roles, allowing the children to exercise their age-appropriate roles. A safe place to develop and experience missed childhood developmental tasks needs to be provided. Be careful not to break down mature coping skills, especially if the family structure is broken. These may be the only way a child from a dysfunctional home can protect him or herself. A shifting of family roles will take time to balance out and test. This may seem precarious and uncomfortable.

Self-mastery and control: Being able to function as a family unit and make healthy decisions not tainted by fear of further abuse is a realistic goal. This means individuals are allowed to make decisions. It means having control physically and emotionally. It means no longer being placed or placing oneself in the victim role. This can be developed by guiding, without controlling, the family and its members through successful decision-making and supporting them through disappointments.

Reconciling the Issues

I have been asked many times how I view my father and those who abused me. In attempting to answer that question, I can say that the view now differs from when I first started this book and varies with each day. That is not to say that I am confused or have ambivalent feelings about them being guilty or not guilty, accountable or victims.

I see this in retrospect as going through a race. When you're in a race, the end seems unobtainable because of all the practice, exercise, injuries and hazards of the road. But when victory is attained, much of the pain and agony is left behind, and it seems to have been well worth the fight. This means working, exercising, stretching, moving toward a goal, having victories along the way.

It has not always been this way for me.

At first I viewed my father with fear and guilt. I had a sense of numbness to what was taking place during the abuse and after the secret was public. Because of his threats and notes, I was torn between fear of him and of what I had done to the family by revealing the secret. That fear remained for many years.

I'm sure I had hidden anger because I had a quick temper and easily argued with people, and was known for my sternness and control. The abuse was often used as an excuse for my social frailties and poor peer relationships. Within the past eight years I have become aware of my anger at what he did to me. The anger became so extreme at times that I had to remind myself when driving to maintain control to avoid hitting someone. I saw my father as having ruined my life, my future—particularly when I had to undergo a hysterectomy.

The fear remained, along with the anger, until I saw my father. He was no longer a giant, but a stooped man, shorter than myself. I was angry that he blamed me and could not take responsibility for his actions. But he became weak in my eyes, and I no longer had to be a fearful little girl.

As the tough front which was protecting me dropped, I could start feeling hurt. For years I had not cried. I don't remember ever crying about my abuse. It was a step in the grieving process. Grieving for my lost childhood, lost family, lost innocence and many other losses followed.

There were times of denial that the incest could have had such an impact on my life. There were other doubts. But these were short-lived. I think then that I was open for healing to take place. As I stopped blaming my father and focused on possible healing for myself, I no longer felt confused with the direction of my life.

Sitting on my bed one night, I recognized many of my struggles as normal not only for incest survivors, but for both females and people in general. I was looking for positive channels for my anger. I realized that if my anger remained focused on my father and other abusers, I could never use my energy for my own healing or to help others. God could not freely do the healing he wanted to do in my life and in others.

I also realized that God was the only one who could change any of my abusers. My concern for them was prayerfully released to God. Now I see my father as someone who once was part of my life. He has affected my life, and I am his blood daughter. But he no longer controls my life in any way. I pray for him at times, but do not think of him daily.

The road to recovery has not always been straight. With each new memory or reminder of abuse that has not been worked through, the grieving returns. This means hurt and healing. But I no longer focus anger on my father. The process is shorter now, as I have experienced comfort in my healing.

At times I see some of my abusers as being both victims and guilty. The younger ones learned the behavior. Some I know were victims of other abusers. Their guilt is for not taking responsibility for their own behavior. I have a sense of pity and sadness for them as well as my father, hoping that someday they will know God's forgiveness and healing.

Yes, the process of healing is time-consuming and stressful, but the resulting peace is well worth it. Philippians 3:13-14 seems to sum it all up: "Brothers, I do not consider myself yet to have taken hold of it. But one thing I do: Forgetting what is behind and straining toward what is ahead, I press on toward the goal to win the prize for which God has called me heavenward in Christ Jesus."

–11–

What
You Can
Do

*W*henever I mention sexual abuse to Christians, reactions vary greatly. Some people are responsive, but many change the subject. People respond: "Oh, does that exist?" or "That doesn't affect Christians!" or "That's an awful subject. How can you stand thinking about it?" When individuals refuse to take sexual abuse seriously, they not only refuse to be part of the solution, they become part of the problem. Their reactions can do great damage to silent abuse victims around them.

But some people are responsive. This chapter is for those Christians who want to help prevent sexual abuse, heal the hurts of past abuses and break the abuse cycle.

I would like to propose some solutions for the problem of sexual abuse and its effect on religious concepts. These are steps that the Christian community can take to accept the responsibility of advocating the cause and needs of abuse survivors and perpetrators. These include evaluation and development in religious material and education, psychological services, leadership training, support services and accountability.

Religious Education

Changes are needed in religious curriculum. I have heard it said that a society's god is based on its authority figure. If this is true, I can understand why we have such differing views of God. But what about the sexual abuse victim, especially if her abuser is her father? And what about the abuser whose path is a well-worn abusive groove? Many distortions or questions can arise.

So how can we make a change in such curriculum? One of the basic ways is by sitting down and listening to those who have been touched by abuse. Listen to their questions and concerns. Give them an un-censoring, unjudgmental audience. Ask questions. Don't treat them as lesser persons for what has happened to them. They can be wonderful clarifiers for teachers. Then use the material with them, testing it and being willing to change. Let them develop material they know will be helpful.

We need to learn the differences between God and a human father. God the Father has set the standards to be followed and is perfect in his ways. An ideal human father will seek to know God's ways as the standard or role model for his fatherhood. This will include instruction in right and wrong, providing a moral standard for the home. He will provide essential two-way communication, listening with an open mind and heart and speaking honestly and openly. Third, he will correct in love as needed, but not when his anger is out of control. Fourth, he will offer encouragement, praise and respect to build godly character. Finally, he will provide and protect. Even an ideal father will not be perfect, but human in functioning.

On the other hand the father of the abused may lack greatly in one of the areas—such as providing healthy knowledge and teaching about normal sexual life, listening to the cause or story behind behavior before disciplining, or providing a safe environment. If the father is the abuser, he may play his father role by demanding control and power, not by following God's standard.

To understand the concept of God from a sexual abuse victim's point of view, one must understand what areas she is struggling with. It usually will be with the attributes of God:

☐ God is our Father. *Her* father is manipulative, inconsistent and secretive. She may not be able to call him "father." She often denies him as a father or wishes that she had another one.

☐ God is love. *Her* father's love is sexual, unclean, painful.

☐ God is all-powerful. *Her* father's power overpowered her.

☐ God is holy. *Her* father's righteousness was hypocritical, so she in turn was made to feel too dirty and unworthy to be approached by true holiness.

☐ God is all-knowing. *Her* father's knowledge only caused her fear.

And if God the Father is different from *her* father, then she must choose between them—and yet somehow obey her parent? How can she trust a God who allows such painful inconsistency? The conclusions made by victims of abuse may seem very irrational, but they are based on conflicting input.

These and many other teachings are extremely difficult for those touched by abuse to understand. If religious leaders and teachers know that sexual abuse exists and how it can distort a person's concept of God, they can make adjustment in the curriculum. They can expect the victim to question religious principles and work from there to clear up any distortion concerning who God is. And an abuser needs to know that he has not been rejected by God for sinning. He is not a failure incapable of changing his ways—with God's help. Curriculum needs to be developed to help in teaching about God. In this way victims and abusers will be helped to heal their wounds.

I had to work through these issues in my own life. At a time when I was struggling with questions, I powerfully experienced God comforting me. The following is part of a poem I wrote about how God spoke to me:

"My child, I love you.
  Look up.
  Trust.
My child, I want you to still be my child—
  don't try to grow up so fast,
    so independent.
You will always be my *child*.
  I will always be your *Father*.
My child, I can heal.
My glory is not seen in your ability to cope with an illness.
My sufficiency can be seen even if there is nothing wrong.
That is not failure on your part—
  I created your mind and your body.
I do not want you to try to control the effect of one on the other.
Spirituality is not shown in anything except
  Jesus Christ being seen in you."

There are other teachings that will help safeguard against the future abuse of other children. It will mean rethinking traditional Christian views. In the past, Christians minimized personal rights and stressed that children should give unquestioning obedience to adults. We need to emphasize rights and needs—especially as they relate to having domain over one's own body. Only then will a girl know she can ask for help and that she can question authority figures who ask her to do something that seems wrong to her.

Part of this process will be rethinking Bible stories. For instance, the biblical example of Ruth has been used to teach young women "how to catch a man." Of course, the story is much more than that. Ruth was a young widow who chose to stay with her mother-in-law after her husband's untimely death. She listened to the wise counsel of an older woman. She was sensitive to the direction of God; she did not act impulsively. Boaz regarded her as a woman of God. He did not push or use her, but waited for her to respond to him.

Joseph and Daniel are also good biblical models. Joseph resisted the sexual advances of Potiphar's wife. Even though he landed in prison, he was true to his convictions. He did not blame his brothers for their abusive behavior, but in time showed evidence of forgiveness and acceptance. And Daniel was taken captive as a young child, but was able to use God's wisdom to remain undefiled against tremendous pressure.

Although the century is different, there is still pressure on young people and adults to conform and lower their standards. Scripture is full of examples of people who were able to withstand such pressure. Adults will need to study together what it means to live as a whole person in the world today. This will entail confronting the sexual needs which are being stimulated by television, movies and magazines—especially if singleness or divorce keep a person from meeting those needs honorably.

Developing Curriculum

The following are curricula concerning sexual abuse which need to be evaluated and developed by Christians:

1. *Educational system:* Christians can have an influence on the curricula in the schools. Get involved in writing, providing, presenting and legislating education on appropriate family and social interaction from kindergarten through graduate school. It will need to be age-appropriate. It may vary from public to private schools. But some things will remain the same.

General areas in which instruction is needed are communication skills, how to choose moral standards and values clarification. It is not unusual to talk with adolescents who are very confused, not knowing right from wrong. They don't have standards for themselves and don't know how to make choices. Another general issue is cause and effect. It is difficult for our "now generation" to look ahead at possible effects of their choices and situations. Safety, trust and honesty all need to be encouraged. Plays, books, puppets, talks can be used with young children to talk about safety and privacy, especially regarding sexual abuse. The use of a police officer is positive to help teach respect and relieve fear of police.

In later years, general sexual information needs to provide clarification and education. Again, plays, books, movies and talks can help with these issues. Assertiveness training should have already started. Parenting skills, sexual identity and sexuality are all issues to cover. Many of these issues are swept "under the rug" so to speak and uninformed individuals end up living miserable lives, having been abused or hiding secrets they thought could never be discussed.

College, seminary and graduate schools could all use courses on abuse. With more people having knowledge of abuse and how to identify and report it, the vicious cycle could be stopped. With classes on parenting, communication skills, assertiveness training and values clarification, perhaps there would be fewer victims and abusers.

Those in helping professions should take specific classes on abuse and have field trips to or internships at places like hospital psychiatric units, youth detention homes, prisons, homes for abused and neglected children and homes for battered wives. Teachers, lawyers, policemen, social workers, doctors, psychiatric workers, dentists and ministers are all people possibly having major contact with abusive situations. They are also in significant positions to provide change. So they need to be trained in specifics. For the most part, they are also mandated to be reporters.

2. Sunday-school, club and camp curriculum: For children, Sunday-school clubs or camps should provide general information about abuse, as the children are not with their parents. The idea is to present biblical principles. In no way are these to alarm, but only to show reality. As a child sees these standards and hears how they are mod-

eled in everyday living, he will be able to see if there is a difference
between what is taught and what occurs in his own home. This will
provoke questions if the teacher or leader stimulates the thinking and
has a listening ear.

Other things to be taught are communication skills and open expression of feelings in an appropriate way. As a child hears the above,
she may feel afraid or threatened if she is living in an abusive situation. The question of potential danger to the child may come to your
mind. If caution is taken and the teacher is a trusted, safe individual,
the child may be provided with hope and help.

Films, art, puppets and role playing are all fun ways of learning.
Clues to abusive situations may be given by children observing or
participating in these learning experiences. Be open, but not quick to
judge. Follow the guidelines outlined in the previous chapter.

Adult Sunday-school curriculum may include the specific issue of
abuse. It will be helpful to have those who have worked through their
abuse and/or professionals share with the group. A panel for open
forum will provide time for questions and answers.

A class for married and single parents, geared toward parenting
skills, will give guidance, new skills and clarification. Provide ample
time for discussion. Discourage judging those who have made mistakes. Bring in professionals to provide extra educational or learning
opportunities.

3. Sermon material: A minister can set the tone for his or her
congregation. I vividly remember a minister remarking that those
with multiple personalities should be treated as though they are pos-
sessed and not be allowed in the church. Yet he also presented some
outstanding sermons on abuse. The material in the sermons on abuse
conflicted with his earlier sermons because multiple personalities are
actually most often a result of severe abuse or trauma.[1]

Sermon material should provide godly principles, our standard for
living. Sermons should teach God's love and justice. They should not
be judgmental. They should provide hope for those who hurt. They

need to present Christianity as a livable way of life, not as perfectionism.

Sermon material can stimulate a caring community of persons who will reach out and help, who will take risks to be different and give instead of taking. Empathic understanding needs to become the norm, rather than being unusual. In our busy world we need to be challenged to give the time it takes to provide a cup of cold water in Jesus' name.

4. Self-help material: Self-help material should be available through the church office or library. Several significant topics would be: parenting skills, communication, assertiveness and abuse. Books, tapes, brochures, classes, movies, videos and one-to-one help are all forms needed.

5. Christian professionals: Christians need to have input into professional writing. It is often hard for us to take risks with our beliefs. But if Christianity, God's principles, are our way of life, they should also be the standard in our professional lives as well. For example, we should be talking about the sanctity of marriage and of life, God's laws, the importance of true spirituality in holistic medicine, honesty in financial matters and so on.

6. Books and articles for adults: There is much literature available today on abuse. There are some books by Christian authors, but some secular authors have presented slanted views of Christianity. We need to flood the media with correct, first-rate material on abuse: hope, help and prevention. This means that Christian authors need to be educated and become knowledgeable enough to provide correct information integrating professional and biblical principles. The materials need to be available for all ages, in all forms and at a reasonable fee. The literature needs to inform and alert about a major issue in society, not simply tickle the ear or senses like pornography or sensual stories. With more people informed, abuse cannot remain a secret.

7. Scripts for radio, television and other forms of multimedia: Secular radio and television have recently presented various programs on abuse. Many of these have given helpful information. Others have seemed to victimize again by sensationalism. Religion on several shows was presented as the culprit behind the abuse. Forgiveness is often misconstrued or misunderstood on these programs. Christian professionals and other Christians who have worked through their abuse are needed on secular programs to give a positive example of God's healing and hope.

Christian television and radio are presenting more programs on abuse. Guidelines need to be used to prevent sensationalism or a soap-opera effect. Professional help should be encouraged as well as reality about the amount of time needed to heal. Hope, help, healing and prevention should be the focus. A caring Christian community across the nation can develop if information is presented in an effective manner.

8. Dramatic works and music: Dramatic works showing the realities of life present signs and effects of abuse. When these are presented on television, in schools, churches or organizations, they can stimulate accountability in the church body. For abuse victims and abusers they provide reality testing.[2]

Music is another key in healing for abuse victims. The secular media is flooded with songs that have abusive lyrics. However, there are a number of songs that tell of abuse and hurt and God's healing. I listened to some of these many times for encouragement, knowing someone knows where I've been, and greater yet, knows God's healing. More such music is needed.[3]

9. Bible study materials: Bible study materials can be used privately or in a group. Specific materials for abuse victims and abusers need to include rebuilding and healing aides. These alone may not provide all the help needed. Professional help in conjunction may be essential. Reteaching the scriptural attributes of God to the heart and mind of the abuse victim will be a challenge, but is greatly needed. Brief devotionals for children and adults will give comfort in specific areas of need for the hurting child within. See the further reading section in appendix two for some helpful resources.

10. Evangelism: One last area to develop is evangelism and Bible
studies for those whom some church members see as reproachable.
Why not consider reaching out to prisoners, delinquents or persons
who are emotionally disturbed, neglected or needy? Opening church
doors for groups of the homeless, alcoholics, drug users, homosexuals
and prostitutes will be a challenge in sharing God's love and resources.
Many victims of abuse will be found in these groups.

Leadership Training

Leaders within the church need to learn about the sexual abuse problem by reading, attending special seminars and listening to those
associated with abuse. Such an education does not come quickly; the
problem is complex. And because the field is comparatively new in
religious circles, leaders should weigh the truth of what they read and
hear, and have professional consultation available. This will help prepare Christian leaders in dealing with those who have been abused.
It will help them develop sensitivity in evangelism by knowing why
some people turn away from God.

The following are sources of education:

1. Abuse survivors and former abusers: Abuse victims present real
life accounts of abuse to help you understand the effects of abuse.
Hear them express feelings and listen to descriptions of resulting
behaviors when the victim has been unable to effectively cope with
the abuse. Learn about the dynamics, the needs and the hopes of those
touched by abuse. Grasp an understanding of the coping skills many
have used to survive, which you can help communicate to others.
Clear up preconceived or misconceived ideas about abuse.

For those telling their stories, opening up will involve risk-taking,
another step in trusting. As they see your caring, concern and openness, it will give them further permission to tell their stories. They
in turn may find new sources of help. Be careful not to exploit by
overusing survivors or pushing them to share beyond their capability
emotionally. Former abusers and family members may also provide

helpful insight for you.

2. Leadership training seminars: Learning to be a leader means learning the team approach. This includes staff selection—carefully screening those who are not willing to work as a team for safety—and perhaps eliminating or being cautious with possible abusers on staff. It will be a place to formulate and activate a team approach to suspected abuse cases in your church or group. It is a place to critique and train for safe leadership, providing role models for those who have not had safe father or mother figures. It should promote accountability. It should be a place for an overview of abuse to be taught for awareness along with how to take action when abuse is suspected. Networking should be developed.

3. Ministerial associations: This is another place for general information to be presented for awareness. It is a place for ministers to glean resources, develop strategies, seek out and set up networking for individual churches and the community. The church body has the right and power to speak out socially, politically and morally. Discreet ways to speak out in public with sensitivity and sensibility should be discussed.

4. Lay leadership: Lay leaders within the church should model caring. They can carefully help the church members to be aware of abusive situations, seek out helping people in the church body and find sheltering homes or families as needed. They can give support and encouragement to those going through the grieving and restoration time after abuse.

Those working with single parents and other singles, children of divorce, homeless people, suicidal persons, and the emotionally or physically ill may frequently come into contact with those who have been touched by abuse. Knowledge is essential for empathetic understanding.

5. Christian education workers: They can teach others how to detect abuse. They can be used as resources in developing curriculum and teaching about abuse to different age groups. They can be resources for teaching parenting classes. They can help clarify difficulties which those touched by abuse might have in understanding religious concepts.

6. *Christian-school staff:* They may be of the same value as church educational staff. As teachers reaching children almost daily, they may have more influence. Once established, they will have information on detection and reporting suspected abuse. They can start at a very early grade level to teach safety to the children. Having parental involvement, the teachers can be role models for leadership and education. Fielding parents' questions about abuse and general issues, such as discipline, will help in preventing abuse. The classroom is a prime place for healthy maturational education, including sexual identity issues. Staff can help parents and others understand normal adolescent individuation, autonomy and intimacy issues. Identifying behavior stemming from abuse, may readily be done by educators knowledgeable about normal developmental stages.

7. *Christian college deans, counselors and residence personnel:* These personnel can be a wealthy resource. With a knowledge of abuse and resulting issues, they may be the first individuals trusted by survivors of abuse. In this safe environment, a survivor may seek help for the first time. Support can be found by them as well as sources for professional help. Educational, support and special interest groups may give first-time information on the reality of abuse, its possible effects and hope for healing, as well as providing positive peer support structure. A knowledge of students or personnel who have been abused may give direction in roommate selection, resolution of acting out behaviors, staff selection and dating issues.

8. *Personnel and candidate directors of Christian organizations and missions:* A keen ear to interpersonal relationships, family history and self-image may give personnel directors clues to a possible history of abuse in a candidate. By dealing with the issues up front, later trauma may be alleviated.

You can be a resource for professional counseling before subsequent issues arise—such as control and trust issues. Awareness in this area may prevent family difficulties on the field and help in team selection. It can provide education to prevent the reoccurrence of the abusive cycle when under stressful situations. Obtaining professional help may delay a candidate who is starting with an organization or going to a field of service, but should serve as groundwork for fruitful service. In no way should one be prevented from working for or serving with a Christian organization because of abuse in his or her background. It may indeed result in increased patience and understanding needed in adverse situations.

9. *Community resources:* There are many community resources available for education, detection and help for those seeking knowledge about abuse. Your local public or school library usually has pamphlets, films and books about abuse. Certain books will list government and local resources to contact. Some schools (especially college and graduate schools) and medical centers have speakers' lists of those who will do presentations at clubs, organizations, schools and churches. A local mental health facility may provide speakers or know of other resources. Some local YWCA's have groups for survivors and may provide speakers or even plays for groups. The police department in some areas presents safety talks at schools. The Department of Children and Family Services and abuse hotlines will provide brochures and booklets. I have always found local librarians very helpful in tracking down needed resources.

Once you start looking for resources in your area, you may be amazed at what you can find. If you find a lack of resources in your area, maybe you can be instrumental in making resources available for others.

Again, I want to stress the importance of confidentiality. I urge you to use your information wisely. For instance, if you know a student or mission candidate has been abused, keep it confidential. Don't assume that others in your group will be equal in their professionalism and confidentiality and make it a general concern. Breaking a trust may do more harm than good.

Psychological Resources

Psychological help is much less taboo in religious circles than it once was. For some it is even a status symbol. For this reason a victim can seek help. For one who feels guilty because of the sexual act itself, she no longer has as much added guilt in seeking out counseling or self-help groups.

Many women will not be comfortable working with a man on this issue because they may feel that the helper is judging them and is again a more powerful male figure. Many times it is best to have the abuser and other family members involved in the counseling because everyone involved needs to be treated.

All psychological professionals should be picked cautiously. Much harm has been done by unqualified counselors who do not sound the depths of the problem or refer cases they cannot properly handle themselves. Some communities may not have a qualified counselor who is also a Christian. A victim can look to the secular community for a qualified therapist if the choice is carefully made.

Some nonreligious counselors assume religion is a protection and an escape. And for some people it is. Freud saw religion as an obsessional neurosis. Jung saw the absence of religion as the chief cause of adult psychological disorders.[4] For some victims, it is the only solace known at a time of crucial need. These are primary issues in therapy. An effective helping professional will need to understand and validate religious concepts, even if he or she does not personally share them.

Finding a therapist or counselor trained in working with abuse cases is becoming easier. I started in the yellow pages—looking at the community resource list. Some sources were not specific to my needs, but I just kept calling and asking for other sources. It was amazing what I found.

The Department of Children and Family Services, abuse and crisis hotlines, hospital emergency rooms or psychiatric units may have agencies' or therapists' names and numbers. Your own family physician or clinic may not only have names, but give a referral to expedite the counseling. County and state agencies as well as Family Service agencies know of local services. Your own community center, school counselor, YWCA and community college may even provide needed counseling services and groups. Don't forget about your church office, ministerial association or the Christian Association for Psychological Studies (CAPS)[5] in seeking resources for counseling. Don't stop with one name, but shop as a consumer for the one best for your situation.[6]

If you feel uncomfortable with a therapist, don't continue. Unfortunately, there are professionals who claim the name of Christ, yet abuse their clients.

Government Services

The church can minister to individuals and families touched by sexual abuse. As openness to the problem comes, help can be developed. It would be ideal to have professional counselors within your church setting. Unfortunately, they are not always available. As the need arises, professional help outside of the Christian community should be used. Private counselors should not be the limit of professional services for you to use. There are helpful state agencies, such as the Department of Children and Family Services (DCFS), family services, school counselors and others.

Christians need to be a positive influence for change in our society. Why not be an active part in advocacy and action? This may be in areas directly or individually touching abuse. For instance, as foster homes are needed, the church family could be one of the healthiest, most supportive places for a sexual abuse victim. You could also volunteer in a home for children where it would not be unusual to see victims of abuse and neglect.

Be a part of support groups as a concerned Christian or survivor. You can be a role model. As a survivor, you can present a challenge for change. Allow others to see that change is possible and how it is possible. If support groups are not available in the community, help get them started. Choose a safe reputable place. Use respectable leaders, carefully chosen. Have team leadership, not just one person. This will provide safety, share responsibility and allow the leadership to see different angles of situations. It will allow for individuality, not dependency.

Seminars for those in all walks of life need to be available because abuse is no respector of persons. If they are not available, you can be instrumental in getting them started. This does not mean you need to present them. Ask for them in schools, PTA's, clubs, organizations, community calenders and on local television. There are knowledgeable persons who can do the presentations. There may be those from agencies available to keep the fee nominal.

Some agencies are now using victim advocates. This is a person, sometimes a survivor or volunteer, who is specially trained to be supportive of an individual victim throughout any legal battle. You could be a volunteer in this program.

Some cities are developing task forces to study the abuse problem in their areas. They are then developing programs to fight the problem. You could be a positive part of this as a survivor and as a Christian. You can provide firsthand experience of help needed in an acceptable manner. You can bridge the gap to local churches, challenging church members to help fight abuse locally.

Speak out locally and nationally by voting. Find out what candidates stand for. Don't be afraid to write them, call them or stop by a local office and let them know what you think. Get involved with campaigns promoting moral justice, and social justice, such as the fight against pornography.

Finally, if you are looking for a vocation, why not consider what you can do in your chosen field to fight abuse? Our government agencies, schools, hospitals and law enforcement agencies all need the positive influence of those who will speak out against abuse. Consider your gifts and the experiences God has allowed you to have, and choose a place where you can be instrumental in change. The rewards will be unlimited.

The Church as Advocate

Support groups and self-help groups within your church family could be very valuable. These would give opportunity for the abused, abusers and their families to work through the treatment issues. Within a church setting where follow-up is available, the extended body of Christ can be models of God's love and care.

Another step toward healing is the provision of support families. A sexual abuse victim often has a distorted picture of men, especially if the problem is incest with her father. Spending time in a healthy family helps a victim to see that all men are not abusers. She can also hear how others relate to God, thereby readjusting her own concepts of God.

Be wise enough to know your limits. Take a team approach to support. Have a plan worked out with your entire staff, including youth leaders and teachers, for reporting suspected and overt abuse to the proper authorities.

Confidentiality is a must. Don't work alone. Have someone you know you can work with who can be trusted. This will prevent blame for further abuse, or the accusation that you told the victim what to say. It will be a shared workload and give a second set of eyes and ears to hear and see what has happened.

What better place is there than the Christian community to help the abuser know the real meaning of forgiveness and healing? I think Matthew 18 speaks to the issue of abuse of children and restorative discipline. Church leaders need to consider how they can approach abusers and challenge them through Christian discipline.

It will take a staff willing to listen, bold enough to face issues, available to spend endless hours in ministering and patient enough to see results. Teamwork is essential. And you must be willing to challenge the abuser to take responsibility.

More than Statistics

In the process of researching and writing this book, I have become increasingly aware of the vast problem of sexual abuse and need for resolution. The grim statistics speak for themselves. But abuse is more than mere statistics, it is real lives touched for eternity. It is lives with scars and brokenness needing mending. It in fact is a death of childhood, death of innocence, an attack on personhood as given by God. It is no respector of persons. It is a severe grief!

Denial of the problem will not wish it away. The historical blaming process needs to stop. The problem is present and needs to be faced and confronted in the present for change. The multitudinal effect is not limited to the victims but extends to family, friends and society as a whole. It also extends from one generation to the next unless its ruthless power is harnessed and redirected in a constructive manner.

We dare not be caught up in blame. The responsibility is not the abuser's alone. If focused on blame, we cannot look ahead to change and do our part as individuals in that change.

We cannot stop with acceptance of the problem of abuse, even if it seems overwhelming. The problem is not insurmountable. Acceptance is not simply forgiving and forgetting. It needs to focus on action with direction. It is empowerment to both the victim and abuser. For the victim it is power to protect and become the complete person God created her to be without victimization. For the abuser it becomes harnessing the destructive power toward constructive change.

No doubt you have experienced some anger as you have read this book. Great! Use that energy to participate in change until the cycle of abuse is broken. You can make a difference.

You may have been a victim. If not of sexual abuse, perhaps you can identify some of the same effects from physical or emotional abuse. Talk with someone you can trust. Seek professional help. Allow yourself healing.

As an abuser, know there is help for you. Seek God's forgiveness.

Allow yourself to be restored to full personhood. This means hard work and letting go of feelings and behavior that have given you a false sense of power and esteem.

Family and friends, please believe the victim. Accept her, support her and allow her to change. Professionals, be patient and supportive, but not overwhelming and controlling. Expect and encourage change.

May this be a fresh beginning of hope, help and healing for those touched by abuse. You may have been abused, but are not abandoned.

Appendix:
Further Reflection
for Those Who
Have Been Abused

Chapter One: A Painful Introduction

1. Write your own story—quickly, without pondering over details, leaving space to add more later. Then go back and add as much more detail as you can. Read it and add to it again and again. (You may wish to use a different color pen or pencil each time you repeat the process.) Also, write down your feelings both as you remember them and as they are elicited when you read your story. It is working through these feelings that will bring healing.

2. Find someone you can trust and tell him or her your story. Verbalizing will provide release. Allow the person to respond, but don't give up if the response isn't what you wanted or expected. Talk about it more *only* if you feel safe.

Chapter Two: What Is Sexual Abuse?

1. Consider your childhood or your present situation—whichever is

appropriate. Are there situations that some might consider abusive?
2. Consider how you interact with your spouse, your children and/or your parents. If you are not clear about what personal boundaries are, discuss it with someone you trust. If, as an adult, you are in an abusive situation, talk with someone to get a realistic perspective on your situation.

Chapter Three: Scapegoats for Abuse
Scapegoats prevent healing and keep the cycle of abuse from being broken. Take a look at the scapegoats you use to deny or distort abuse. What do you need to do to get back on target and combat abuse?

Chapter Four: The Climate for Abuse
1. Describe your family and home in either words or a picture. What does it say about safety, communication, feelings and your family's foundation and basis for home? Discuss it with someone you trust.
2. Describe the place in which you were abused. What would need to be changed to make it safe?
3. Look through old family photos to get a realistic view of your family. The photos may jog some partial or lost memories. Describe your family roles and how they played into the abuse. Can they be changed?
4. If you are an adult, do you see those same family roles being played out in your present living situation? What needs to change to prevent an abusive situation?

Chapter Five: Characteristics of Abusers
Describe, draw or make a clay figure of your abuser. Talk about him with someone you trust.

Chapter Six: Characteristics of the Abused
1. Describe yourself as you were before, during and after the abuse using words or pictures. Describe what you would like to be like.

2. Make a list of your strengths and explain how you can use each one with specific problems.

Chapter Seven: The Dilemma of Disclosure
If you are being abused now, talk about it with someone you trust. It is never too late to stop the cycle and get help.

Chapter Eight: The Other Victims
1. Within your family, discuss roles and the part each member plays in keeping communication open and the living situation safe.

What do you think is a realistic future for your family? How can you help make sure this takes place?

2. Consider those you know who have been touched by abuse. Consider how you can help them through the crisis and provide a caring role model in the future.

Chapter Nine: Healing for the Abused
1. Realize that healing is possible. Find someone, possibly a professional, whom you can trust, and get started.

2. Take a look at each of the treatment issues suggested by Sgroi. Think about what your difficulties are in the areas of trust, anger, self-esteem and so on.

What would you like to change in each area? Take steps to make changes, getting help as necessary.

Chapter Ten: Healing for Abusers and Families
1. Remember the clay figure that you made of your abuser? Use it to get in touch with your anger toward your abuser.

2. Voice your feelings in a letter (which you do not need to send) to your abuser. You may want to read your letter to the clay figure, an empty chair which represents your abuser, o r in a role play with someone.

Now the process of forgiveness can begin.

Chapter Eleven: What You Can Do

1. Set one goal—whether large or small—that you can achieve this year in the fight against abuse. Challenge others in your church and community to set their own goals or work with you.

2. Prayerfully consider who else you can give this book to, or place a copy in a library so that others can get information and help.

Notes

Chapter Two: What Is Sexual Abuse?

[1]Brian G. Fraser, *The Educator and Child Abuse* (Chicago: National Committee for Prevention of Child Abuse, 1977), p. 3.

[2]Ibid.

[3]Ibid.

[4]National Center on Child Abuse and Neglect, *Child Sexual Abuse: Incest, Assault and Sexual Exploitation* (Washington, D.C.: U.S. Department of Health, Education and Welfare, August 1978), p. 2.

[5]*Basic Facts about Sexual Child Abuse* (Chicago: National Committee for Prevention of Child Abuse, 1982).

[6]David Finkelhor, *Sexually Victimized Children* (New York: The Free Press, 1979), p. 28.

[7]Gary May, *Understanding Sexual Child Abuse* (Chicago: National Committee for Prevention of Child Abuse, 1978) p. 7.

[8]Ibid., p. 8.

[9]As quoted from DeFrancis, *Sexual Abuse of Children* by the National Center on Child Abuse and Neglect (Washington D.C.: U.S. Department of Health, Education and Welfare, August 1986), p. 5. See also a comparison study in David Finkelhor, *Sexually Victimized Children,* p. 155.

[10]Suzanne Sgroi, *Handbook of Clinical Intervention in Child Sexual Abuse* (Lexington: Lexington Books, 1982), p. 13.

[11]Vincent J. Fontana, *Dealing with Sexual Child Abuse* (Chicago: National Committee for Prevention of Child Abuse, 1982), p. 1.

[12]Ibid.

[13]Judith Herman, *Father-Daughter Incest* (Cambridge: Harvard University Press, 1981), p. 13.

[14]Phone conversation of September 1, 1987 with the American Humane Association, Denver, Colorado. It takes two years to compile such statistics.

15"Profile of Child Abuse and Neglect," an information sheet compiled by the National Center on Child Abuse and Neglect.

16American Humane Association, November 8, 1985, as used by the *Literature Review of Sexual Abuse* (Washington, D.C.: U.S. Department of Health Education and Welfare, 1986), p. 3.

17Herman, *Father-Daughter Incest,* p. 68.

18Diana Russell, *The Secret Trauma* (New York: Basic Books Inc., 1986), p. 10.

19Finkelhor, *Sexually Victimized Children,* pp. 53, 56, 75.

20R. L. Johnson and D. K. Shrier, "Sexual Victimization of Boys: Experience at an Adolescent Medical Clinic," *Journal of Adolescent Health Care,* 6(5) (1985):372-76.

21Florence Rush, *The Best Kept Secret: Sexual Abuse of Children* (New York: McGraw-Hill, 1980).

22I used Herman's study as a basis for comparison, as I felt her figure was low. See Herman, *Father-Daughter Incest.*

Chapter Three: Scapegoats for Abuse

1Herman, *Father-Daughter Incest,* p. 9.

2Jeffrey Moussaieff Masson, *The Assault on Truth* (New York: Penguin Books, 1984), pp. xx, 263, 267.

3Ibid., p. 136.

4Ibid., p. 129.

5Ibid., pp. 198, 200, 276.

6Ibid., p. 112.

7Ibid., pp. 132, 136, 196, 198.

8Ibid., p. 200.

9Herman, *Father-Daughter Incest,* p. 12.

10Ibid., p. 14.

11Ibid., p. 16.

12Ibid., p. 18.

13Jakob and Wilhelm Grimm, *Grimms' Tales for Young and Old,* trans. by Ralph Manheim (Garden City, N.Y.: Doubleday, 1977), pp. 3-6.

14Ibid., pp. 196-98.

15Ibid., pp. 352-56.

16Rush, *The Best Kept Secret,* p. 17.

17Ibid., p. 19.

18David K. Walters, *Physical and Sexual Abuse of Children* (Bloomington, Ind.: Indiana University Press, 1975), p. 9.

Chapter Four: The Climate for Abuse

1Grace H. Ketterman and Herbert L. Ketterman, *The Complete Book of Baby* and *Child Care for Christian Parents* (Old Tappan, N.J.: Fleming H. Revell, 1982), pp. 140, 468-72.

[2]Letha Dawson Scanzoni, *Sex Is a Parent Affair* (New York: Bantam Books, 1982), p. 186.

[3]Ibid., p. 200.

[4]Herman, *Father-Daughter Incest,* p. 39.

[5]Sgroi, *Clinical Intervention,* p. 30.

[6]Ibid., pp. 18, 29.

[7]Finkelhor, *Sexually Victimized Children,* p. 25.

[8]Ibid., p. 26.

[9]Ibid., p. 27.

[10]Ibid.

[11]A. Nicholas Groth, *Men Who Rape* (New York: Plenum Press, 1979), pp. 142, 186; Sgroi, *Clinical Intervention,* p. 228; Fraser, *Educator,* p. 9.

[12]Sgroi, *Clinical Intervention,* p. 15.

[13]Ibid., p. 15; Fraser, *Educator and Child Abuse,* p. 9.

[14]Sgroi, *Clinical Intervention,* p. 218; Finkelhor, *Sexually Victimized Children,* p. 118.

[15]Finkelhor, *Sexually Victimized Children,* p. 149.

[16]Walters, *Physical and Sexual Abuse,* p. 125.

[17]Groth, *Men Who Rape,* p. 154.

[18]Fraser, *Educator and Child Abuse,* p. 10.

[19]May, *Sexual Child Abuse,* p. 18.

[20]Sgroi, *Clinical Intervention,* p. 219.

[21]Dr. Alvere Stern, Administrator, Illinois Department of Alcoholism and Substance Abuse in a seminar, January 1990.

[22]Finkelhor, *Sexually Victimized Children,* p. 22.

[23]Groth, *Men Who Rape,* p. 97.

[24]Charles P. Barnard, "Alcoholism and Incest: Improving Diagnostic Comprehensiveness," *International Journal of Family Therapy* 5 (Summer 1983):136-144.

[25]Herman, *Father-Daughter Incest,* pp. 71, 111.

[26]Sgroi, *Clinical Intervention,* p. 16.

[27]J. Weiss, E. Rogers, M. Darwin and C. Dutton, "A Study of Girl Sex Victims," *Psychiatric Quarterly* 29(1) (1955):1-27.

[28]Sgroi, *Clinical Intervention,* p. 243.

[29]Ruth S. Kempe and C. Henry Kempe, *Child Abuse* (Cambridge, Mass.: Harvard University Press, 1978), p. 68.

Chapter Five: Characteristics of Abusers

[1]Hank Giarretto, Child Abuse Treatment/Training Program, San Jose, California, in phone conversation, January 1988.

[2]Linda Tschirhart Sanford, *The Silent Children* (Garden City, N.Y.: Anchor Press, 1980), p. 97; Tamar Cohen, "The Incestuous Family Revisited," *Social Casework: The Journal of Contemporary Social Work* March (1983):154-161; Herman, *Father-Daughter Incest*, p. 78; David Finkelhor, *Sexually Victimized Children*, p. 26.

[3]Sgroi, *Clinical Intervention*, p. 229; Finkelhor, *Sexually Victimized Children*, p. 30.

[4]Sanford, *Silent Children*, p. 96.

[5]Herman, *Father-Daughter Incest*, p. 81; Finkelhor, *Sexually Victimized Children*, p. 26.

[6]Groth, *Men Who Rape*, p. 146.

[7]Walters, *Physical and Sexual Abuse*, p. 146.

[8]Sgroi, *Clinical Intervention*, p. 87; Groth, *Men Who Rape*, p. 154; Herman, *Father-Daughter Incest*, p. 76.

[9]Finkelhor, *Sexually Victimized Children*, p. 21; Sanford, *Silent Children*, p. 87.

[10]Patrick Carnes, *Out of the Shadows* (Minneapolis, Minn.: CompCare, 1983), p. 9.

[11]Ibid., p. 54.

[11]Martin Levine and Richard Troiden, "The Myth of Sexual Compulsivity," *The Journal of Sex Research* (25 August 1988):347-363.

[13]Ibid.

[14]Vincent DeFrancis, "Protecting the Child Victim of Sex Crimes Committed by Adults" (Denver, Colo.: Denver American Humane Association, 1969), p. 69-70, as used by May, *Sexual Child Abuse*, p. 10.

[15]Diane DePanfilis, *Literature Review of Sexual Abuse* (Washington, D.C.: Clearinghouse on Child Abuse and Neglect Information, August 1986), p. 7; Russell, *The Secret Trauma*, p. 96; Herman, *Father-Daughter Incest*, pp. 14, 109; Finkelhor, *Sexually Victimized Children*, p. 63; Sanford, *Silent Children*, pp. 234-62.

[16]This anonymous personal account was given to the author.

[17]Herman, *Father-Daughter Incest*, pp. 91, 116; Russell, *Secret Trauma*, pp. 126, 194.

[18]Groth, *Men Who Rape*, p. 151.

[19]Paul H. Gebhard, John H. Gagnon, Wardell B. Pomeroy, Cornelia V. Christenson, *Sex Offenders* (New York: Harper & Row, 1965), pp. 222, 677.

[20]Russell, *Secret Trauma*, p. 254.

[21]Rush, *The Best Kept Secret*, p. 164.

[22]*Highlights of Official Child Neglect and Abuse Neglect and Abuse Reporting* (Denver: American Humane Association, 1987), p. 19.

[23]Groth, *Men Who Rape*, pp. 141-43.

[24]Groth, *Men Who Rape*, pp. 154-60.

[25]Russell, *Secret Trauma*, p. 297.

[26]DePanfilis, *Review of Sexual Abuse*, p. 5.

[27]Ibid., p. 8; Finkelhor, *Sexually Victimized Children*, p. 88.

[28]Sgroi, *Clinical Intervention*, p. 231.

[29]Herman, *Father-Daughter Incest*, p. 8. Kee MacFarlane, Jill Waterman, *Sexual Abuse of Young Children* (New York: The Guilford Press, 1986), p. 9.

[30]Russell, *Secret Trauma*, p. 297. Sgroi, *Clinical Intervention*, p. 231; MacFarlane, *Sexual Abuse*, p. 9.

[31]Sgroi, *Clinical Intervention*, p. 177-189; Christine A. Courtois, "Studying and Counseling Women with Past Incest Experience," *Victimology: An International Journal*, 5(2-4) (1980): 327; Ellen Cole, "Sibling Incest: The Myth of Benign Sibling Incest," *Current Feminist Issues in Psychotherapy* (1982):79; Russell, *Secret Trauma*, p. 270; Herman, *Father-Daughter Incest*, p. 94.

Chapter Six: Characteristics of the Abused

[1]Rebekah Riskin, "Hiding," unpublished poem used by permission of the author.

[2]David Finkelhor and L. Baron, "Risk Factors for Childhood Sexual Abuse: A Review of the Evidence," unpublished report of the Family Violence Research Program, University of New Hampshire, February 1985, p. 6, as reported in United States Department of Health and Human Services, *Literature Review of Sexual Abuse* (Washington, D.C., 1986).

[3]American Association for Protecting Children, *Highlights of Official Child Neglect and Abuse Reporting 1985* (Denver: American Humane Association, 1987), p. 19.

[4]Vincent DeFrancis, *Protecting the Child Victim of Sex Crimes Committed by Adults* (Denver: American Humane Association, 1969) as used by Finkelhor, "Risk Factors," p. 68.

[5]Herman, *Father-Daughter Incest*, p. 84.

[6]Having specific evidence of sexual abuse would make validating sexual abuse, and thus treatment, more successful. Unfortunately, it is not that easy. To show how complex the effects of the abuse are, I have listed some of the typical characteristics clinicians and researchers have found in those who have been abused.

For further information see Suzanne M. Sgroi, *Clinical Intervention*, p. 40. MacFarlane and Waterman, *Sexual Abuse*, pp. 101ff. David Muram, "Rape, Incest, Trauma: The Molested Child," *Clinical Obstetrics and Gynecology* 30(3) (September 1987):754-61.

[7]Herman, *Father-Daughter Incest*, p. 79.

[8]As told to the author by anonymous sources.

[9]Robin Warshaw, *I Never Called It Rape* (New York: Harper & Row, 1988),

p. 53.

[10]David Finkelhor, *A Source Book on Child Sexual Abuse* (Beverly Hills, Calif.: Sage Publications, 1986), p. 151.

[11]M. A. Fossom and M. J. Mason, *Facing Shame* (New York: W. W. Norton, 1986), as used in Christine Courtois, *Healing the Incest Wound* (New York: W. W. Norton, 1988), p. 311. See also Lenore E. Auerbach, ed., *Handbook on Sexual Abuse of Children* (New York: Springer Publishing, 1988), p. 95.

[12]Jean Benward and Judianne Densen-Gerber, "Incest as a Causative Factor in Antisocial Behavior: An Exploratory Study," *Contemporary Drug Problems,* 4(3) Fall 1975: 326.

[13]Herman, *Father-Daughter Incest,* p. 119.

[14]National Committee for Prevention of Child Abuse, *Basic Facts about Sexual Child Abuse* (Chicago: National Committee on the Prevention of Child Abuse, 1985), p. 1.

[15]Mitchell Ditkoff, "Child Pornography," in *The American Humane Society* 16(4) 1978.

[16]Sam Janus, *The Death of Innocence* (New York: William Morrow, 1981), p. 169.

[17]Roberta A. Hibbard and Donald P. Orr, "Incest and Sexual Abuse," *Seminars in Adolescent Medicine* 1(3) (September 1985):160.

[18]Irving Stuart and Joanne Greer, eds., *Victims of Sexual Aggression* (New York: Van Nostrand Reinhold Co., 1984), p. 251.

[19]Chicago *Tribune,* Sunday, June 24, 1984, Sec. 1, p. 14.

[20]A. W. Burgess, "Research on the Use of Children in Pornography" and J. W. Dillingham and E. C. Melmed, "Child Pornography: A Study of the Social Sexual Abuse of Children," papers presented at a briefing on Child Pornography Projects funded by the National Center on Child Abuse and Neglect, Washington, D.C., December 18, 1982.

[21]Russell, *The Secret Trauma,* p. 160.

[22]As presented by A. Nicholas Groth, Sexual Assault Conference, Governors State University, June 18, 1984.

[23]Henry Giarretto, "A Comprehensive Child Sexual Abuse Treatment Program," *Child Abuse and Neglect* 6(3) 1982.

[24]Russell, *The Secret Trauma,* p. 158.

[25]Ibid., p. 160.

[26]Ibid., p. 162.

Chapter Seven: The Dilemma of Disclosure

[1]Louise Armstrong, *Kiss Daddy Goodnight* (New York: Pocket Books, 1978), p. 7.

[2]Herman, *Father-Daughter Incest,* p. 129.

[3]Suzanne J. Smither, *Incest Task Force* (Urban Rape Crisis Services, 1982),

p. 85.

[4]Charlotte Vale Allen, *Daddy's Girl* (New York: Berkley Books, 1980), p. 56.

[5]Jean Renvoize, *Incest* (London: Routledge & Kegan Paul, 1982), p. 43.

[6]Sgroi, *Clinical Intervention* (Lexington, Mass.: Lexington Books, 1984), p. 129.

[7]Ibid., p. 113.

[8]Ibid., pp. 17, 117.

[9]Smither, *Incest Task Force*, p. 85.

[10]Sgroi, *Clinical Intervention*, pp. 23, 29.

[11]Russell, *The Secret Trauma*, p. 358.

[12]Ibid., p. 369.

[13]This study is based on Mahler's developmental psychology which focuses on the first three years of life. Although this is only one of many personality theories, I think Amanat's work is helpful.

[14]Stuart and Greer, *Victims of Sexual Aggression*, p. 43.

[15]Ibid., p. 97.

[16]David Finkelhor, *A Source Book*, p. 109.

[17]Armstrong, p. 16.

[18]Finkelhor, *A Source Book*, p. 106.

[19]Kenneth J. Gruber, Robert Jones and Mary Freeman, "Youth Reactions to Sexual Assault," *Adolescence* 17 (67), (1982):541.

[20]James, p. 146.

[21]Sgroi, *Clinical Intervention*, pps. 31, 184.

[22]Renvoize, *Incest*, p. 64.

[23]Herman, *Father-Daughter Incest*, p. 132.

[24]Sgroi, *Clinical Intervention*, p. 19.

[25]Renvoize, *Incest*, p. 43.

[26]Smither, *Incest Task Force*, p. 90.

[27]Sgroi, *Clinical Intervention*, p. 18.

[28]Ibid., p. 22.

[29]Stuart and Greer, *Victims of Sexual Aggression*, p. 62.

[30]Susan Brownmiller, *Against Our Will* (New York: Bantam Books, 1975).

Chapter Eight: The Other Victims

[1]Dr. Nicholas A. Groth, Sexual Assault Conference, Governors State University, June 18, 1984. Also see Dr. Nicholas A. Groth, *Men Who Rape*, New York: Plenum Press, 1979.

[2]John White and Ken Blue, *Healing the Wounded* (Downers Grove, Ill.: InterVarsity Press, 1985).

[3]Barbara Star, *Helping the Abuser* (Family Service Association of America: New York, 1983, pp. 12-14, 39-47.)

[4]Giarretto, *Child Abuse and Neglect*, p. 265.

Chapter Nine: Healing for the Abused

[1]John G. Finch, "Some Thoughts on Integrating Psychology into the Christian Faith," unpublished manuscript, May 1975, p. 5.

[2]Sgroi, *Clinical Intervention,* p. 142.

[3]Ibid., p. 109.

[4]Christine A. Courtois, *Healing the Incest Wound* (New York: W. W. Norton, 1988), p. 202.

[5]Mike Lew, *Victims No Longer* (New York: Nevraumont Publishing Co., 1988), p. 95ff.

Chapter Ten: Healing for Abusers and Families

[1]Roberta A. Hibbard and Donald P. Orr, *Seminars in Adolescent Medicine,* p. 160.

[2]Nicholas A. Groth, William F. Hobson, Kevin B. Lucey and Joyce St. Pierre, "Juvenile Sexual Offenders: Guidelines for Treatment," *International Journal of Offender Therapy and Comparative Criminology,* p. 269.

[3]Carnes, *Out of the Shadows,* p. 133.

[4]Ibid., p. 137.

Chapter Eleven: What You Can Do

[1]The most frequently reported relationship between multiple personalities and abuse is in cases involving incest with sadism. See Frank W. Putnam, *Diagnosis and Treatment of Multiple Personality Disorders* (New York: Guilford Press, 1989), p. 45ff.

[2]"Unshackled" is a radio program by Pacific Garden Mission that does this well. Also see the video "Ripped Down the Middle" by Dale and Juanita Ryan, available from Twenty-One Hundred Productions, a division of InterVarsity Christian Fellowship, Madison, Wis.

[3]Some examples of singers whose music I have found helpful are Myrna White, Joyce Landorf, Amy Grant, and Steve and Annie Chapman.

[4]Jeeves, 1978.

[5]CAPS has a national directory available. You can write or call for more information: Christian Association for Psychological Studies, P.O. Box 628, Blue Jay, Calif. 92317, (714) 337-5117.

[6]I do not endorse any one therapist or source. It is too difficult to keep up with this ever-changing profession. Additionally, there is no way to know what the professional's moral or spiritual approach and accountability is like.

Further Reading

There are many books available on the subject of abuse. The following list of books builds on the subjects found in these chapters. These books all contain information that you should find helpful and challenging, but I do not endorse any particular book.

First-Person Accounts of Abuse

Allen, Charlotte Vale. *Daddy's Girl.* New York: Berkley Books, 1980. True story of a child's ordeal of shame.

Botkin-Maher, Jennifer. *Nice Girls Don't Get Raped.* San Bernardino, Calif.: Here's Life, 1987. True story of a woman raped at knifepoint which covers how to deal with and protect yourself from rape.

Edwards, Katherine. *A House Divided.* Grand Rapids, Mich.: Zondervan, 1984. True story of abuse and God's healing.

Hester, Glenn; Nygren, Bruce. *Child of Rage.* Nashville: Thomas Nelson, 1981. Story of a boy who overcame abuse during a troubled adolescence.

Janssen, Martha. *Silent Scream.* Philadelphia: Fortress, 1983. Sensitive poetry written by incest victims.

Marshall, Catherine. *Christy.* New York: McGraw-Hill, 1967. Novel about life in the Tennessee Hills which includes abuse.

Quinn, P. E. *Cry Out: Inside the Terrifying World of an Abused Child.* Nashville: Abingdon, 1984. A boy who survived abuse.

Ricks, Chip. *Carol's Story.* Wheaton, Ill.: Tyndale, 1981. Story of incest through victim's eyes and her struggles in growing up.

Smith, Nancy Anne. *All I Need Is Love.* Downers Grove, Ill.: InterVarsity

Press, 1977. Account of a missionary who experienced hysterical paralysis
that revealed childhood trauma.

VanStone, Doris. *Dorie: the Girl Nobody Loved.* Chicago: Moody Press, 1979.
Moving true account of a girl who was abandoned and abused, but experienced God's healing and became a responsible adult.

Waters, Ethel. *To Me It's Wonderful.* New York: Harper & Row, 1972. Personal story of a woman whose life began with rape and abuse, but whom
God used to touch lives through her acting, singing and speaking.

What Is Sexual Abuse?

Hancock, Maxine; Mains, Karen Burton. *Child Sexual Abuse: A Hope for
Healing.* Wheaton, Ill.: Harold Shaw, 1987. Overview of abuse with help
for adult victims.

Hyde, Margaret O. *Sexual Abuse.* Philadelphia: Westminster Press, 1984.
Brief overview of abuse.

Miller, Alice. *For Your Own Good.* Trans. by Hildegarde and Hunter Hannum.
New York: Farrar, Straus, Giroux, 1983. Ways of childrearing which may
be considered abusive and lead to violence.

Monfalcone, Wesley R. *Coping with Abuse in the Family.* Philadelphia: Westminster Press, 1980. The subtlety of abuse and how to change.

Peters, David B. *A Betrayal of Innocence.* Waco, Tex.: Word, 1986. Overview
of abuse by a family counselor and child protective services worker.

Vredevelt, Pamela; Rodriguez, Katheryn. *Surviving the Secret.* Old Tappan,
N.J.: Revell, 1987. Explores how to identify and heal abuse with insight
from Scripture.

Wilson, Earl D. *A Silence to Be Broken.* Portland, Ore.: Multnomah, 1986.
Overview of abuse and God's healing.

Scapegoats

Rush, Florence. *The Best Kept Secret.* New York: McGraw-Hill, 1980. Ex-
plore historical patterns of blaming for present-day abuse.

Climate for Abuse

Beattie, Melody. *Codependent No More.* New York: Harper/Hazelden, 1987.
How to recognize and get out of codependent situations.

Chapian, Marie. *Mothers & Daughters.* Minneapolis, Minn.: Bethany House,
1988. Building communication between mothers and daughters by focusing on individual uniquenesses.

Gage, Joy P. *Broken Boundaries, Broken Lives.* Denver, Colo.: Accent Books,
1981. Boundaries and responsibilities for parents.

Gris, J. Bruce. *What to Do When the Family Hurts.* Wheaton, Ill.: Tyndale,
1982. Encouraging help to rebuild broken families.

Landorf, Joyce. *Irregular People.* Waco, Tex.: Word, 1982. How to deal with the difficult people in your life.

Michaelsen, Johanna. *Like Lambs to the Slaughter.* Eugene, Oreg.: Harvest House, 1989. Shocking book about children and the occult.

Characteristics of Abusers
Groth, A. Nicholas. *Men Who Rape.* New York: Plenum Press, 1979. Looks at the emotional and psychological factors behind men with sexually abusive lifestyles.

Trobisch, Walter. *The Misunderstood Man.* Downers Grove, Ill.: InterVarsity Press, 1983. Understanding the male psyche.

Characteristics of the Abused
Sgroi, Suzanne M. *Handbook of Clinical Intervention in Child Sexual Abuse.* Lexington, Mass.: Lexington Books, 1982. Readable book by a professional addressing many areas in the complex assessment and treatment of sexual abuse.

Stuart, Irving R.; Greer, Joanne G. *Victims of Sexual Aggression.* New York: Van Nostrand Reinhold, 1984. Scholarly, but readable, book about treating abuse victims of both sexes and of all ages.

Walker, Lenore. *Handbook on Sexual Abuse of Children.* New York: Springer Publishing, 1988. Compilation of up-to-date information on assessment and treatment issues for the professional.

Disclosure
Augsburger, David. *Caring Enough to Confront.* Glendale, Calif.: Regal, 1973. Learning to honestly express feelings, especially anger, and build trust.

Powell, John. *Why Am I Afraid to Tell You Who I Am?* Los Angeles: Argus Communications, 1969. Being honest with yourself and others as part of building self-esteem.

Help for Families
Alsdurf, James and Phyllis. *Battered into Submission.* Downers Grove: InterVarsity Press, 1989. The problem of wife abuse in Christian homes.

Dobson, James C. *Love Must Be Tough.* Waco, Tex.: Word, 1983. Help for families in a crisis.

Martin, Grant. *Please Don't Hurt Me.* Wheaton, Ill.: Victor Books, 1987. The cycle of abuse between generations with reference to Christian homes.

The Healing Process
Augsburger, David. *Seventy Times Seven.* Chicago: Moody Press, 1970. Learning to forgive.

Bass, Ellen; Davis, Laura. *The Courage to Heal.* New York: Harper & Row, 1988. An extensive self-help guide for women who have been abused.

Guernsey, Dennis. *Sometimes It's Hard to Love God.* Downers Grove, Ill.: InterVarsity Press, 1989. How to build a relationship with God when life has been tough.

Landorf, Joyce. *The Fragrance of Beauty.* Fullerton, Calif.: Victor Books, 1973. Classic on building inner beauty. Deals with fear, worry, anger, inferiority and forgiveness.

Leman, Kevin; Carlson, Randy. *Unlocking the Secrets of Your Childhood Memories.* Nashville: Thomas Nelson, 1989. Practical help in working through childhood bitterness and unlocking forgotten memories.

Lew, Mike. *Victims No Longer.* New York: Nevraumont Publishing, 1988. Deals with incest and other sexual abuses of males.

MacDonald, Gordon and Gail. *If Those Who Reach Could Touch.* Chicago: Moody Press, 1984. Practical guide to developing empathetic communication.

Needham, David C. with Larry Libby. *Close to His Majesty.* Portland, Oreg.: Multnomah, 1987. A refreshing and challenging look at walking close to God.

Payne, Leanne. *The Broken Image.* Westchester, Ill.: Crossway, 1981. Understanding the homosexual identity crisis.

Sell, Charles. *Unfinished Business.* Portland, Oreg.: Multnomah, 1989. Help for adult children from dysfunctional families involving alcoholism and emotional, physical and/or sexual abuse.

Smedes, Lewis B. *Forgive & Forget.* San Francisco: Harper & Row, 1984. Forgiving those who have hurt you.

Trobisch, Walter. *Love Yourself.* Downers Grove, Ill.: InterVarsity Press, 1976. A small, practical book on self-acceptance and dealing with depression.

Whitfield, Charles L. *Healing the Child Within.* Deerfield Beach, Fla.: Health Communications, 1987. Discovery and recovery for adult children from dysfunctional families.

Wilkes, Peter. *Overcoming Anger.* Downers Grove, Ill.: InterVarsity Press, 1987. Practical book emphasizing God's power to change human frailties.

Wilson, Sandra. *Released from Shame.* Downers Grove, Ill.: InterVarsity Press, 1990. Personal perspective on understanding and recovery from dysfunctional families for adult children.

Educating Children

Berry, Jo. *Alerting Kids to the Danger of Sexual Abuse.* Waco, Tex.: Word, 1984. An illustrated book for parents to use with small children with a brief section of information for parents.

Carl, Angela R. *Good Hugs and Bad Hugs.* Cincinnati, Ohio: Standard, 1985. Workbook emphazing stranger abuse for young children with some Scripture and general information.

Dobson, James. *Preparing for Adolescence.* Ventura, Calif.: Regal, 1979. A workbook for parents to use with children in opening up difficult topics for communication.

Heitritter, Lynn. *Little Ones Activity Workbook.* Young America, Minn.: Little Ones Books, 1983. Activity book to use with young children in discussing good touching and "what if" situations.

Sanford, Doris. *I Can't Talk about It.* Portland, Oreg.: Multnomah, 1986. Beautifully illustrated, unintrusive book about sexual abuse for young children.

Wilder, E. James. *Just between Father & Son.* Downers Grove, Ill.: InterVarsity Press, 1990. Story of how one father took his son on a camping trip to discuss puberty and the facts of life, including an account of how he taught his sons to protect themselves from sexual abuse and a section on dating girls who have been sexually abused.

Taking Action

Baker, Don. *Beyond Forgiveness.* Portland, Oreg.: Multnomah, 1984. Healing through church discipline.

Fortune, Marie Marshall. *Sexual Violence.* New York: Pilgrim Press, 1983. Ethical and pastoral perspective on sexual violence.

Heitritter, Lynn; Vought, Jeanette. *Helping Victims of Sexual Abuse.* Minneapolis, Minn.: Bethany House, 1989. Details on organizing and running a group for adult survivors of sexual abuse.

Ryan, Dale and Juanita. Life Recovery Guide series. Downers Grove, Ill.: InterVarsity Press, 1990. Bible study guides for group or personal use. Titles include *Recovery from Abuse, Recovery from Shame, Recovery from Dysfunctional Families, Recovery from Distorted Images of God, Recovery from Bitterness, Recovery from Addictions, Recovery from Codependency* and *Recovery from Loss.*